The Strain of Shackles

By

DeVan Faye Brittenum, Nom de Plume

Deborah Faye Martin

Evelyn Martin-Woods

and

York Martin III, Esquire

ISBN: 1501054880
ISBN: 13: 9781501054884

Beneath the words of fiction written inside **The Strain of Shackles**, the truth unravels from nonfiction. Have the names been changed to protect the guilty? The characters in **The Strain of Shackles** are fictional. The literary profile of each person does not depict the lives, events, names or words of any human being living or deceased. These characters and scenes are figments of the author's imagination. Any resemblances to actual scenario or persons are coincidental. **The Strain of Shackles** utilize strong adult language.

DEDICATION

The Strain of Shackles is dedicated to women who
are incarcerated in our nation's penal institutions.
Stay strong, and continue to pray. We are grateful for our
grandparents, Willie and Lois Greenwood, for their love
and support. Thank you to our cousins, Mildred and Ollie,
for their encouragement. Special acknowledgements are
extended to our father, York Martin Jr. We love you!

Wintrell Ray, York III, and DeVan Faye

To my Brother, York

We were blessed with the ability to write novels. I thank God that our mother imparted this gift to us. You taught me the publishing business, and you showed me how to query agents. Your knowledge helped me to become a published author with guest appearances on News Channel 3: Good Morning Memphis with Alex and Marybeth, Fox News Channel 13 twice, NBC News Channel 4 in Nashville, TN, News Radio 960 KZIM in Cape Girardeau, Missouri, the Bev Johnson Show on WDIA Radio, and ABC News Channel 24 with Amy Speropoulous twice. Thank you, Gerald Malone, for arranging the interviews for me on ABC News. I appreciate Freddie Milton for taking a media picture of me at ABC News. York, I could not have achieved these feats without your expertise in the publishing industry. I am proud of your accomplishment with your screenplay entitled "Pimpology: The Macking Game".

With Love,

DeVan Faye Brittenum, Nom de Plume

and

Deborah Faye Martin

.

Consider it pure joy, my brothers, whenever you face trials of many kinds because you know that the testing of your faith develops perseverance.

James 1:2-4

CONTENTS

PROLOGUE

In the 21st century, African-Americans lynch fellow Blacks at a greater magnitude than the Ku Klux Klan. Eve's genealogy stems from Master Dick Johnson's plantation in Mississippi, and her life's hurdles evolved on the Deaderick Plantation in Orange Mound. Eve lived in the first African-American residential area in the South after the Civil War. Eve overcame many adversities as a teenage mother. *The Strain of Shackles* documents the manner in which Blacks utilize the doctrines of Willie Lynch against other African-Americans on the job, in spiritual institutions, and in the educational arena. The acronym BBB is the newfangled phrase used in reference to racial bigotry within the Black ethnological environment. Black, Bold, and Bigots are words designed to convey the evils of genocidal racism. African-Americans use the word Nigger as a term of endearment within our own social circle, but the "N" word becomes offensive when uttered from the lips of different ethnic groups. Shackles on the mind-set of some individuals hinder the growth of a nation. Moreover, Eve suffered condemnation while worshipping at Mt. Malachi CME Church. Eve's daughter, Faith, was the target of Willie Lynch's Color Theory. Faith's marriage into the Billingston family caused her to endure the Willie Lynch doctrine on her job. Eve faced a a journey through the Criminal Justice Center when her daughter was incarcerated in jail. Even though Faith's cellmate was White, they formed an esprit de corps. A degree of comradeship formed between the cellmates from different ethnic backgrounds. *The Strain of Shackles* is the most controversial novel of the 21st century.

Chapter 1.

YOUNG LOVE

In 1947, Newton and Eve were the best of friends. They lived in a section of Memphis, Tennessee known as Orange Mound. Historical data cites this neighborhood as the first African-American dwelling environment in the South after the Civil War. According to historiographers, John George Deaderick sold land on his plantation to Izey Eugene Meacham in 1890. Hence, this section of Memphis was affectionately called Orange Mound Tennessee. The Mound was a state within a state. The nomenclature representing the color orange was derived from the Osage orange shrubs adorning the Deaderick Plantation. This swanky little subdivision exercised the power of self-reliance. The residents in the Mound didn't venture outside of the neighborhood for much of anything. The neighborhood developed a commercial district with a Gas Station, a laundry for cleaning clothes, a school to educate the children, and two stores. The inhabitants were doctors, lawyers, entrepreneurs, teachers, and laborers. Occasionally, they would board the bus to go downtown. At this time in our country's history, Blacks rode on the back of the bus. All of the major department stores were downtown, and the Jews owned all of the stores like Goldsmith's, Sheinberg's, and Lowenstein's. Eve's parents travelled to Memphis in 1926 after the annexation of Orange Mound. From 1865 to the 1900's, Memphis flourished after the Civil War to a notable American city. Eve had a rich family lineage connected to Master Dick Johnson's Plantation in Mississippi. The slaves called him Ma Stick because they could not pronounce his name. His wife was Mistress Susan Johnson. Eve's forefathers arrived in America on the crowded Moon Tavern slave ship which docked at Moon Landing in Tunica, Mississippi. Master Dick Johnson bought several slaves from the auction block at Moon Landing. He rode the slaves on the back of his wagon from Tunica past the Coldwater River through Choctaw Ridge into Panola County. Ma Stick owned about 164 slaves, and the little piccaninies were also counted as Master's property. Slavery emphasized the idea of complete ownership. In the slave quarters, the black family lived in a one or two room log cabin with dirt floors. Lazy slaves were cast into the pen. Nigger pens were built to shelter darkies like hogs in a slop pen. Blacks housed in the pens were auctioned off to the highest bidder. At the slave auction sale, all of the young niggers would be sold. According to Oral Tradition, Ma Stick was a very good master. The slaves received rations of food every Saturday morning, and he clothed them for every season of the year. Ma Stick's goodness of heart surfaced when the Ku Klux Klan rode onto the plantation to purchase their robes. Old Miss designed robes for the KKK, and the white plantation owners secured her seamstress services. Several slaves worked in the garden planting flowers. One Klansman grabbed Nigger Elijah by the limb, and he nearly broke his arm. The slaves were afraid of them, and no one uttered a mumbling word. The Klan members were known to kill and beat colored people unmercifully. Ma Stick appeared suddenly with a shotgun in hand, and he demanded that the Klan release his property. Master Dick Johnson never let the paddy rollers whoop his colored folks. Ma Stick was rich as hell, and nobody challenged him: black or white. An account of Eve's ancestry revealed Mammy as the Lady's Maid. The official records document Mammy as Eve's great-grandmother. This stereotypical black woman played a vital role in Ma Stick's household. She enslaved work for Mistress Sarah while nursing the family's children. She raised Master Harold Johnson and little Missy Celia from birth. The majority of Mammy's duties were related to relieving the mistress of the drudgery work that is associated with child care. Her main role was to help the mistress with household tasks. She was next to the mistress in authority, but she was of a lower status. Mammy even had the authority to give orders to everybody in the house. The matriarch of the slaves possessed an air of refinement, and she was highly intelligent. Mammy learned her ABC's from the Master's children. When they came home from school, the slave maid listened intensely to them read. As they read aloud, Mammy mimicked the phonic pronunciation of the words. An analysis of the flowing handwriting of the white children taught Mammy to scribble her name. The slave code legally banned the teaching of reading to victims of servitude. Therefore, Mammy shrewdly hid her ability to read and write. In olden days, slaves lived in a specified milieu south of the Mason-Dixon Line. This boundary geographically separated the free states from the slave states. In 1861, newsmongers spread rumors about an invasion from a northern military operation. Master Johnson, a tall stately gentleman with a long beard, lounged on his mansion's front porch. The little black children strolled upon Ma Stick's porch elegantly greeting him with a courtesy.

"Good morning, Master," they said in perfect accord. In non-standard English, the children questioned their Master about idle rumors.

"I member hearing folks say peoples coming." Ellen recollected.

"Um! Um! That's what all them say," Ma Stick affirmed.

"Master, you put woolen clothes and heavy shoes on my feet every winter. I ain't got a thing in the world to worry 'bout. You is a good master." Betsy said.

"Who told you about the military?" The Master questioned.

"I jest can't member. I done told you all I know, Master." Ellen said.

"The grapevine said folk coming through town gone tell us 'bout freedom." Amos stated.

"Um! Um! That's what all them say. The information is unverified. That gossip is hearsay." Master Dick said.

"Papa say slavery wasn't that bad with him and mama." Betsy said.

"I tell yo, Master Stick, yo sho treat us slabs fair." Ellen stated in dialect.

"I'm proud to own you. You are good workers." Master Johnson admitted.

"Chile ain't nothin happening," Sadie said.

"They say de call Yanks. I'm tell in' you the truth." Amos said.

"Is that true, Ma Stick?" Betsy inquired.

"I suppose. That information is circulating all around town." Master Dick said.

"Now jes lis'en. You say yo' wants tuh talk tuh Ma Stick." Betty said.

"You will always have a home on my Plantation. You are welcomed." Master Dick convinced his slaves. The Yankees penetrated the premises of the Confederates in 1861. The invasion by the Union was the topic of conversation in Panola County. Rumors spread about the Yanks fighting down in Vicksburg. Confederate General Earl Van Dorn from Holly Spring, Mississippi hindered the Union's victory in the battle of Vicksburg by destroying the enemy's war materials. The clash of arms between the North and the South filled the plantation owners with horror. The bloodthirsty Yanks confiscated the slaveowners' personal items. Master Dick Johnson refused to relinquish his valuables. He instructed the slaves to dig a grave in his family's cemetery. The slaves lowered a coffin into a six-foot grave with a large sum of money, jewelry, silver candle holders, gold, and silverware. The casket hid his wealth from view. Amos left the Johnson's Plantation in quest of freedom. He evaded traveling to Virginia because of the antebellum tales about the first slaveholder of African birth. The slaves on Master Dick's plantation revealed the legends surrounding the first Black slave owner from Virginia. Anthony Johnson was a free Negro in the 1600's. He was not related to Master Dick Johnson by birth or servitude. The similarity in name is coincidental. The slaves told about the cruel treatment of Master Anthony Johnson towards a fellow African. As a Black slave owner, he denied Casor his freedom. Amos' odyssey led him through the Underground Railroad to the Burkle house on Second Street in Memphis, Tennessee. Jacob Burkle sat at his desk peering from wire-rim glasses while reading when he heard a tap, tap, tap on the window pane. Glaring into the darkness of the night, he made eye contact with Amos. The abolitionist of German descent provided a safe haven for him to escape from the perils of slavery. He covertly opened the door, and he lowered the runaway into a small cellar filled with ten escaped slaves. The shackles of slavery vanished as Amos descended the stairs into the dark, dreary, damp cellar. Since Memphis was the largest slave market in the Mid-South, the Burkle Way-Station provided a secret safe haven for slaves. Burkle's risky venture endangered his life while helping Africans in their pursuit for freedom. The modest one-story white frame slave-haven was located near the banks of the Mississippi River. Because of the Burkle Estates close proximity to the Mississippi River, the slaves built an underground tunnel leading to the river. The silty loess clay soil around the Burkle property was the perfect tunnelling substance without the need for many supports.

Crawling through the dusty tunnel to the escape route for slaves on the Mississippi River, Amos was snuggled on a steamboat inside a cotton bale. The steamboat sailed down the Mississippi River past Cairo, Illinois into Canada. When Memphis succumbed to the Union forces early in the Civil War, Amos became a free man. After the war, the slaves were awarded freedom. The niggers were forced to leave the comfort of the plantation. When Big Daddy moved from the Delta in Mississippi, he purchased a Plot of land in the Mound. According to statistics, the developers sold land in the 1800's from the Deadcrick Plantation in 25 foot lots for less than $100.00 dollars. Big Daddy built a nice seven room frame house for his family. It was nicely furnished, and it was always clean. The patriarch of Eve's family was the proud father of two daughters and one son. Eve's sister, Lily, was two years older. Her brother, Winston, was seven years younger. Her mom conceived Winston during the Change. Big Daddy provided a good life for his family. Since Madea matriculated at Mississippi Industrial College in Holly Springs, Mississippi, she taught First grade and Third grade in Tunica before moving to Memphis. After relocating to Memphis, Big Daddy suggested that she attend to household duties while he worked to provide a good lifestyle for the family. Eve was from a middle class African-American family. Her father worked in the mailroom for Illinois Central Railroad, and her mother was a Homemaker. Her mom contributed to the household by using her skills as a seamstress in order to make fashionable attires for family and friends. Mistress Sarah taught Mammy how to do housework, all kinds of sewing, and cutting patterns. Mammy imparted seamstress skills to Madea and her siblings. Madea would buy her children's shoes, socks and underwear to match their pretty homemade outfits. Newton's genealogical history unveils the Chickasaw Indian tribe as his family's ancestors. The Chickasaw clan traced their ancestry through the mother's pedigree. The matrilineal historical descent of the Chickasaw tribe was recorded by the Dawes Commission between 1898 and 1916. Newton's grandmother spoke a Chickasaw language called Muskogean. The "Trail of Tears" shed grief on the lamenting heart of the Chickasaw's spirit. Nevertheless, his grandmother did not relocate during the Great Removal of 1830. Grandma Itanale remained in Marshall County in Mississippi. During the Civil War, Newton's ancestry formed an allegiance with the Confederate Army. Nathan Bedford Forrest, a general in the Civil War, was instrumental in gaining the devotion of the Chickasaw Indians because he lived in the Marshall County area. By means of a Flash -Forward literary technique, the ability to foresee the future of Nathan Bedford Forrest in Memphis reflects doom. Known as having been a prominent figure in the foundation of the Ku Klux Klan, Nathan Bedford Forrest's image wore a blemish of hatred for future generations. The massacre of Black soldiers in the Battle of Shiloh, Tennessee placed a stain on Forrest's image. The "wizard of the saddle" whizzed through the soldiers' camp during the Battle of Shiloh. The rallying-cry for the African-American soldiers executed by Nathan Bedford Forrest echoed into the year 2015. With a guilty conscious in 1871, Nathan Bedford Forrest denounced any affiliation with the Ku Klux Klan before the Congressional Committee. However, the Bluff City Council members pictured the historical figure as a symbol of hatred. In the fullness of time, the Bluff City Council members voted to remove the remains of Confederate General Nathan Bedford Forrest from a municipal park. The Tennessee General Assembly's passage of the Heritage Protection Act of 2013 inherited the power to preserve history. What is a country without a history? A Flashback literary technique captures events during the Civil War era. In 1870, the Western part of the county became Benton County after the Civil War. Aba' Binni li' (our God) preordained the Itanale descendants to reside in Ashland, Mississippi within Benton County. Grandma Itanale married an African name Reverend Johnathon Hinton. However, Chickasaw culture insisted on denying people of African/Indian mixed ancestry. Reverend and Grandma Itanale brought forth six children. Grandpa Hinton suffered death. While standing under a tree during a storm, lightning struck him. Itanale's oldest daughter was seventeen when Reverend drew his last breath. After the demise of her father, Sally left Ashland, Mississippi with her mother, two brothers and three sisters. She travelled across states to flee from the sharecropping lifestyle inflicted on her after slavery. Her brother, John, endured the strain of shackles. He was relentlessly beaten. The sum of Grandma Sally's sharecropping experience prompted her to escape from the ills of slavery. Plantationism forced sharecroppers to escape to Memphis or to the North area of the country. The family sojourned from Mississippi, and they migrated to Collierville, Tennessee. Itanale and her family sought refuge with the Ashwin Cherokee Indian tribe in Collierville, Tennessee. Ashwin and Itanale spoke in the basic Cherokee language.

Chereeka Language Interpretation

Chokma	Hello	(Itanale)
Ga do de tsa do a	What is your name?	(Ashwin)
a-yu-wi-ya Cha La Gi	I am Cherokee Indian	(Itanale)
tsi lu gi	Welcome	(Ashwin)
wa do	Thank you	(Itanale)
Do hi qu u	How are you?	(Ashwin)

Chereeka Language Interpretation

| Os di | fine | (Itanale) |
| Ne he na ha | and you? | (Itanale) |

Newton's father worked for Southern Railroad, and his mother was a homemaker as well. Newton was the second son of six children. Papa Ashwin had two sons and four daughters. Papa lived in Collierville, TN, but he moved to Memphis after he married Sally. Newton and Eve lived in close proximity to each other. Their parents' houses were a couple of streets away. It was easy for them to fraternize with each other. They were friends since first grade. Now at sixteen, they became lovers. They attended Wildcats High School, and they were enrolled in several classes together. In fact, Eve often completed Newton's homework because he worked part-time at Rainbow Lake on Lamar Avenue. Rainbow Lake was a resort that offered tennis and fine dining for the elite. Newton and Eve became a couple. One night, Newton invited Eve on a date. They walked down Park Avenue to Handy Theatre. Since segregation was prevalent, African-Americans were excluded from every aspect of white society. Thus, Newton and Eve viewed the movie at an all-black theatre. "Odd Man Out", a drama about Gang War Crimes, played on the big screen. This thriller captivated the audiences' attention. The black and white film was directed by Carol Reed. James Mason, Robert Newton, Cyril Cusack, and Kathleen Ryan starred in the movie. Newton went to the concession stand for a minute to purchase popcorn and soda. After the movie, they strolled down Airways toward Orange Mound Park. They could swing and swim for recreation, but Newton didn't want to swing or swim. He wanted to swing Eve's legs around his back, and he wanted to let his sperm swim towards her eggs. Standing near the Monkey Bars, Newton the third was conceived. Fear engulfed Eve's mind. She feared telling her parents about the unwanted pregnancy. During the 1940's, society ostracized young ladies who became pregnant out-of-wedlock. Eve was devastated at the thought of being a teenage mom. She confided in her sister.

"Lily, I missed my Period. I haven't had a menstrual cycle in months. I wish my cycle would come. What am I going to do?" She asked.

"You better pray." Lily advised her on a spiritual level.

"Girl! I need to pray, and I need to see a few drops of blood." Eve said.

"What are you going to do about school?" Lily inquired.

"I will keep going to school. Hopefully, no one will notice." She said in an attempt to conceal her pregnancy.

"You want to be able to hide your pregnancy forever. Your stomach will get bigger." Lily warned.

"I know. I'll think of something." Eve stated while thinking of a cover-up scheme. Eve knew that her secret was safe with Lily. Lily would never betray her confidence. The first blush of morning arrived in a flash. The morning peeked through the window, and Eve arouse at the crack of dawn. The young maiden washed her face, bathed her impregnated body, brushed her teeth, and combed her hair. Madea prepared breakfast, and they consumed a hearty meal. News of a recent happening circulated around the Wildcat's Den. The buzz around campus spread the rumor of a house party hosted by Hannah and her sister Francis. Eve's best friend Lois informed her about the party. Hannah and Francis distributed invitations to the social affair to their friends. Eve and Lois' names didn't appear on the guest list, but the love of their life's names headed the list. Hannah's heart throbbed for Newton, but Eve was known around campus as his lady. Lois' competition was Hannah's best friend Wilma. Since Lois' parents owned the local Hamburger joint, they strolled to Hamburger Haven to discuss the party.

"We can't go to the party. We weren't invited." Lois surmised.

"We need to spy on them." Eve suggested.

"How do you plan to spy on them? You know Hannah's mother runs a Transit House."

"What's a Transit House."

"It's a house where men and women meet to have sex. Honey, she gets paid to rent rooms to people for sexual activities." Lois explained.

"Well, they won't linger the night of the party. The festivities will only be for the children." On the night of the party, the rain drizzled on their heads while listening to the music blasting. They stepped in a big puddle of mud.

"Gosh! Let's go! I got mud on my new shoes," Lois said. Finally, they left the area. Confidentially, Newton called his sister Lucille in Michigan. He confided the secret about impregnating Eve.

"Hello!" Lucille answered the phone in a jovial tone.

"Hello, Lucille! I need to have a little talk with you. This is personal. I've messed up my life. Eve is pregnant. Don't tell momma. Keep this pregnancy hush- hush". Newton asked Lucille to keep the pregnancy under cover.

"How many months pregnant is Eve?"

"She is three months."

"Newton Junior, you won't be able to conceal this pregnancy forever. The baby will come into the world six months from now. Eve needs prenatal care; she needs to visit the doctor's office."

"Lucille, keep my secret."

"I'm glad that you confided in me, but you need to consort with momma. Are you still working?"

"Yes! I'm earning money. So, I don't have to acquire a livelihood. I'll provide for my child's needs." Newton Junior revealed his financial circumstances.

"I'm glad that you can make ends meet."

"I'll talk with you later." Newton Junior said.

"Okay! Bye!"

"Bye!" Lucille called Momma Sally long distance to spill the beans.

"Momma, how are you?"

"I'm fine, Lucille. It's good hearing from you. How are your sons?"

"Brandon and Ronald are growing fast. They will manage the funeral home with Walton when they get older." Lucille envisioned.

"I believe Walton is looking forward to working with his sons." Momma Sally said.

"I need to discuss something important with you concerning Newton Junior. He swore me to secrecy, but I need to be true to life."

"What's wrong with Newton Junior?"

"Newton Junior created a baby with Eve. Momma, Eve is pregnant. They are expecting a baby."

"Oh! No! They are only sixteen years old. Does Eve's mother know about the pregnancy?"

"No! Mrs. Greene doesn't know yet. Eve hasn't told her parents." A meeting of the minds united Newton Junior and Eve. Mental telepathy transmitted a desire for companionship. Newton decided to pay a visit to Eve. Madea interrupted them.

"Eve, I need you to purchase some items at the market. Get some turnip greens, mustard greens, sweet potatoes, and flour." Madea handed her the money.

"Okay! Madea!" Eve agreed while taking the money. "Newton is going to the market with me."

"That's fine. I'll clean the chicken while you're gone." Eve picked fresh greens and selected the other items on the list. In olden days, parents taught responsibility to their children. Young people were dependable, and parents relied upon them to go shopping. At long last, Newton's mother unveiled the truth. The clandestine conception of a baby uncovered Eve's pregnancy.

"Hello, Mrs. Greene! This is Sally Mimmus: Newton's mother."

"Hello Sally. Newton went to the market with Eve. I'll tell him to call you as soon as he returns."

"I'm calling to talk with you. Eve is pregnant. Newton confessed their secret to my oldest daughter. We need to arrange a family conference. What day will be convenient for your family?"

"Sunday evening after church will be the best time for our family." Madea decided. "I appreciate you telling me. Eve hasn't said a word."

"What time should we arrive?"

"Let's meet about 4:00 o'clock P.M."

"We will see you Sunday." The span of time drifted toward the families' meeting. Newton's parents appeared promptly at the appointed time for the conference.

"We expect Newton to have good intentions. He will take responsibility for impregnating Eve. When my daughters got pregnant, the young men married them." Mrs. Mimmus stated.

"We appreciate your candour. We don't believe in bearing illegitimate children. They are young, and they are still in high school. Her education is important. Eve will not stop getting her education. She will continue going to school." Madea said emphatically.

"Madea," Eve interrupted. "I don't want to go back to Wildcat's Den."

"Eve, it is mandatory that you get a high school diploma. You have a responsibility, and you need to be financially able to support your child. You must go to school." Madea demanded.

"May I go to Watson High?"

"Watson is downtown." Madea concluded. "How are you going to get to school every day? Your father works at night. He won't be able to drive you to Watson."

"Madea! I can ride the bus."

"We will make arrangements for you to continue your education. Our main concern is your welfare." Madea assured Eve.

"This is our grandchild, and both families will work together." Big Daddy stated. In the course of time, the families went to the Court House in order to secure a marriage license. From the hills of Mississippi to the flat lands of the Delta, Newton and Eve's paths crossed into holy matrimony. Higgins was a cozy place in the Mound for teenagers to mingle after school. The young people gathered to fellowship. Higgins did not sell alcoholic beverages to teenagers. Eve's clique was teetotallers. They enjoyed hamburgers, hot dogs and soda in Higgins' social environment. Newton's friend, T.L. Thomas, managed this teenage hang-out, and everyone from Wildcat's Den patronized the club. Newton would meet Eve at Higgins when he left work. Their friends teased Eve about her big stomach.

"You and the bundle can sit over here." William said in jest.

"It is not enough room for that load." T.L. teased Eve because her pregnancy showed. Eve laughed, and she sat down to enjoy the entertainment. Newton played the following songs on the jukebox: Honky Tonkin', It's Stormy Monday but Tuesday Is Just as Bad, and That's All Right. Hannah's mother came into Higgins in search of her daughter. Mrs. Fonda Billingston confronted Eve, and she said.

"Oh! You are pregnant. You are a cow having a calf."

"That is a cruel statement for a mother of daughters to make. You are disrespectful." Newton came to Eve's defence.

"It's my calf, and I'm proud to be this baby's father." Newton admitted with pride. No one cared about Mrs. Billingston's point of view because everyone in the Mound knew about her house of ill repute. The young couple left Higgins en route for home. Upon arriving home, Eve was confronted with a philosophical lesson that initiated a depth of thought. Mrs. Sally Mimmus was a profoundly perceptive woman. Worldly wisdom guided her with the ability to discern the truth about maintaining a stable relationship. She presented a thought-provoking question to Eve.

"If your mother and Newton were drowning, who would you save?"

"I would save my mother." Eve answered honestly.

"You should save Newton Junior." Mrs Mimmus delivered a practical outlook on marriage to Eve. "When you marry, you must leave you family and cleave to your husband. You and your husband have become one."

"I love my mother. I couldn't let my mother drown." Eve confessed.

Chapter 2.

THE BETRAYAL

The direction of events in Eve's life glided her gracefully into enrolling in LeMoyne-Owen College, and she worked part-time at Happy Land Kindergarten. Teaching four- and five-year old's basic skill, social behavior by playing games, exercises, and simple handicrafts in preparation for First grade was the deciding factor in the selection of Eve's college major. She majored in Elementary Education. Meanwhile, Newton gained a better paying job at Humko Oil Refinery. Since their financial situation increased, the young couple rented an apartment in the Project Complex on Boston Street in Orange Mound. While cohabitating, Eve gave birth to Faith. Newton the third inherited the name New Baby to differentiate him from Newton Senior and Newton Junior. Life appeared perfect on the surface, but infidelity placed a stumbling block in the marriage. Newton received flattering attention from a neighbor living in the Projects. Ironically, she was married to a tall, handsome, light complexion gentleman with curly hair. Humko planned a company picnic at Fuller's Park in South Memphis. While wooing Newton, the seductress wiggled her way into attending the picnic. To transport the family to the picnic,

Newton borrowed his friend William's car. Eve, New Baby, Faith, and Grandma Sally boarded the vehicle. The concubine occupied the front seat with Newton and his mother. The sitting arrangement was a disrespectful maneuver by the sleazy slut. The wife should have been seated next to her husband, but Eve sat quietly in the back with her children. Eve delighted in the social affair. The Humko employees treated her with kindness. Newton's lover, on the other hand, was totally ignored while sitting alone looking bewildered. The children played games, and they engaged in a conversation with their peers. At the end of the picnic, Newton placed the key in the ignition. The ignition failed to set the car in motion. The jalopy produced a humming sound. The intruder grew impatient with the mechanic's ability to fix the automobile. She hustled a ride with another gentleman. Finally, Newton repaired the vehicle, and the family rode home without the floozy. The young couple moved from the Projects to a Duplex on Hanley Street. Two years later, the number of children rose to three when Eve gave birth to her second son. She named him Rayan which means favored by God, and the name Rayan originated from the Arabic language. Once they moved from the projects, the courting did not cease. Newton cheated with Edna Bee. She seized a chance to court Newton. He continued to betray Eve by breaking the rules of marriage again. The present juncture dictated that Eve's family travel to Mound Bayou, Mississippi because of the hospitalization of her grandmother. Grandma Savannah was greatly stricken with some affliction. Her frail, feeble, body suffered from some malady. Eve made arrangements with her next-door neighbor to baby sit with the children.

"Mary, I've got to go to Mound Bayou, Mississippi. My grandmother is gravely ill, and my mother wants us to go with her to the medical center. Will you keep my children? I'll be gone for several hours."

"Sure! I will be glad to keep them. They are well-mannered, and I enjoy keeping your children."

"Mary, I really do appreciate your help. Newton will be home later. Please let him know that I've gone to Mississippi."

"I will, Eve. Don't worry. I will take very good care of the children."

"I know that you will take good care of my children. Thank you!" Newton reached his homebound destination. Mary informed him about his wife's trip to Mississippi.

"Eve went to Mound Bayou. Her grandmother is under the weather. The poor, old lady is sickly, and she is ailing. Eve will return late tonight. I have the children; I'm baby-sitting. Since you are home, I'll send them home, now."

"Mary, could you keep the children a while longer. I planned to meet my friend and his lady at Billingston's Café, but I'll invite them over to the apartment."

"Sure, Newton. I'll keep them. I've already fed them dinner. They are not a problem." Mary volunteered to keep the children a while longer. Newton fabricated a false story by stretching the truth about his friend's relationship to Edna Bee. He attempted to pull the wool over Mary's eyes. He concocted some cock-and-bull story about Edna Bee's loving relationship with his friend. Realistically, Edna Bee was the young man's sister not his lover. She possessed no sense of right and wrong. She stealthily entered Eve's house to court her husband. The romantic counterplot unfolded when Edna Bee and her brother visited the apartment. Mary sat on the front porch while the children played in the yard. The deceitful rendezvous was exposed when Mary recognized Edna Bee and her brother. She heard the rumor about the romantic relationship between Edna Bee and Newton. The misrepresentation of the mistress unmasked a deceptive plot to continue an illicit affair in Eve's house. Newton's wife showed up unexpectedly. Eve emerged on the scene in the mist of mischief. She was unaware of the relationship between Newton and Edna Bee. Therefore, she greeted the guest in an amicable fashion. Her friendly feelings welcomed the couple to her home. Eve talked about her trip, and she discussed the health issue of her grandmother. Mary brought the children home. Newton discussed the group's plans for the evening.

"We are going to the nightclub. The crowd hangs-out at Billingston's Café on Airways. Honey, I want you to go with us. You haven't been out to a nightspot in years. You have maintained the house, attended college, and cared for our children. You deserve a good time. Let's club together." Newton desired his wife to accompany him to the club.

"I don't have anything to wear." Eve said.

"You've got a pretty outfit to wear." Mary intervened. "Why don't you wear that black skirt with the matching multi-colored blouse?" The neighbor was aware of the deceitful circumstances, and she placed a stumbling block in Edna Bee's romantic plan. "I'll keep the children. They always go to bed at eight o'clock, anyway. I will watch television. Go! Have a good time." Mary encouraged Eve to enjoy the evening. The couple put in an appearance at Billingston's Café. Edna Bee's lackluster attitude placed a dark cloud on the evening fun. Jealousy captivated her spirit, and Edna Bee showed ill-will toward the couple's relationship. Abruptly, she left the Juke Joint without saying a word.

"Where is your lady?" Eve asked Edna Bee's brother.

"I think she went to her friend's house?" He said in an attempt to hide the deception. Newton and Eve continued to party, and the brother sat in the club looking stupid. After work one evening, Newton volunteered to walk the children to Orange Mound Park. The family promenaded with a steady pace to the park. However, Newton had an ulterior motive for taking his children to the public park. He secretly planned to meet Edna Bee in an undisclosed location. Newton and Edna Bee surreptitiously sealed their scheme to meet by using the children as a shield. She came on the scene with five children. The children entertained themselves. The playful action engaged the five boys in horseplay while the three little girls amused themselves on the Swing set. At the end of the play date, the couple continued their fling at Edna

Bee's apartment. Newton departed about seven o'clock because his children always went to sleep at 8:00 o'clock every night. Faith experienced the time of her life. The fun-loving time lingered in her mind.

"Momma! I had a good time. Daddy took us to the playground. We played with Edna Bee's children. Then, we went to their house. They live in a white house. It was two houses joined together." The child informant enlightened her mother about Newton's illicit affair. At five years old, Faith described the home-wreckers place of residence.

"I'm glad that you enjoyed yourself. Have you ever visited that house before today?" Eve quizzed.

"No ma'am! That was my first-time visiting Ms. Bee's house." Faith confessed. The unveiling of the romantic revelation leaked the location of Eve's nemesis' place of residence. A woman's instinctive feelings make her aware of infidelity. The sixth sense sends information to her. Eve received immediate cognition when Theresa came to babysit.

"I just saw Newton," Theresa disclosed.

"Where did you see him?" Eve questioned.

"I saw him going down Spotswood toward Josephine Street. Don't you have a friend who lives on Josephine?" Theresa inquired.

"Yes! My friend, Carolyn, lives on Josephine." Eve surmised.

"Why don't you visit her? I'll keep the children."

"Great! I will visit Carolyn. I could use some free time. I needed to go to the library in order to complete an assignment, but I'll go chat with Carolyn." Eve travelled to Carolyn's house. Once she reached the destination, Carolyn greeted her with exuberance. She was tickled with pleasure to welcome an unannounced guest. Carolyn talked a great deal about trivial things, but Eve enjoyed the garrulous person. During the decline of day, Eve walked home. On her journey home, Eve's inductive reasoning ability observed Newton's old car parked at an apartment. Walking toward the Duplex apartment, Eve recollected a mental picture of the white houses connected together that her daughter described. She pounds on the door with a rapping noise. Edna Bee flung the door open revealing Newton sitting on the sofa in full view. Her husband was up to his usual shenanigans. With permission to enter her enemy's home, Eve asked to look at the children.

"Hi! How are you doing?" Eve asked pleasantly while gaining access into the apartment.

"I'm fine." Edna Bee said.

"Do you have any children?" Eve asked a leading question.

"Yes! Here are my children," Edna Bee revealed proudly. "These are my two sons, and these three children are my sisters." She disclosed.

"I'm eager to learn the paternity of your children." Eve showed her curiosity. "I'm just nosy. I'm prying into the hereditary traits of your children. My mind is at ease. All of your children are dark complexion. Since Newton is light complexion, they can't be his children." Eve's inquiring mind relaxed.

"No! My children's father lives in Tunica, Mississippi." Edna Bee explained.

"Thank you!" Eve said while making her departure. A parent should use prudence when courting on a spouse. Newton learned a valuable lesson: never take your child with you on a date. Newton drove slowly alongside of her begging Eve to ride in the car. Tearfully, Eve told Madea about confronting Newton in his lover's apartment.

"Madea, I found Newton visiting his lady's house. She is the same woman in my apartment when I arrived home from Mound Bayou. They are having an affair. I looked at her children. I wanted to see if they resembled Newton, but they weren't his children."

"Eve, you were wrong for entering your competition's house. She could have killed you, and the police would call it self-defense. They would say that you were trespassing. Never enter the other woman's house again. That's dangerous." Madea warned.

"I won't go to her house again, but she had the unmitigated gall to come to my house." Eve recalled. Springtime leaped success in Eve's educational accomplishments. She successfully completed the Spring Semester in college. For the time being, Eve could relax from studying. Nadolyn urged her to attend the movie theatre. They walked past Billingston's Café en-route to Handy Theatre. The young ladies decided to play a couple of songs on the Juke Box. Upon entering the club, Eve recognized Newton sitting with Edna Bee. Eve lost control of herself. The marriage partner went amok. An argument ensued which ended in a violent rage. Eve plunged into a battle with Edna Bee. The waitress in the club called the police. Two men in the club beckoned Eve and Nadolyn to flee across the street to Palm Garden Café.

"Wow! You beat her ass. Hurry! Go over to the police first." The young man advised. "Tell the police that Newton and Edna Bee attacked you." The glint and glitter of the patrol car's blue lights flashed while arriving on the scene.

"Officer, I need help. My husband and his lover jumped on me in the club." Eve explained. "We've got three children at home, and his woman caused a conflict in the club. The big scrimmage injured me. I want to file a Police Report."

"What is your husband's name?"

"Newton Mimmus is my husband. Her name is Edna Bee." The officer went to Billingston's Café, and they arrested the couple. The officer cuffed and stuffed Newton and Edna Bee. They were transported to jail. Finally, the judge set a bond. The bond was paid, and they were freed from incarceration. The couple separated after the suspenseful event at the club. While residing at Madea's house, the issue of life insurance on Eve's children was addressed.

"Eve, Mr. Anderson came by to get money on your life insurance policies on the children. You need to keep the insurance. It is financial protection against loss of life." Madea said.

"Mr. Anderson worries me about paying on the policies. He is a cool white dude, but I've been running short on cash." Eve explained.

"I understand your financial situation. A single mother with three children has a financial challenge, but you must pay your insurance."

"Okay Madea! I'll give Mr. Anderson the money this evening." A difficult dilemma deposited more stumbling blocks in Eve's path. A dreadful incident caused a life full of hardship and heartache. A birthday celebration at Mrs. Hawkins's house turned into a dramatic direction. All of the children in the neighborhood attended the birthday party across the street from Madea's house. They enjoyed the treats and festivity. Once the party ended, Lily's three sons and Eve's three children crossed the street safely. Around the corner from Madea's residence, Club Carnes host alcoholic guzzlers. The club's patrons tossed down liquor like water. Doris decided to drive under the influence of alcohol. In a state of total intoxication, her reflexes slowed to a snail's pace. The rooaarrr of the engine's noise echoed for miles. Varoom! Varoom! The tires screeched with a high pitch sound as the car turned the corner at a fast speed. The motorist drove in a rapid motion through a residential area. The automobile moved expeditiously as she sped along Clover Street. The magnitude of the vehicle's velocity exceeded the legal limit. On the spur of the moment, Rayan walked across the street in search of more birthday treats. The three-year-old unfortunately stumbled upon a dangerous situation. He became the victim of pathological drunkenness. On a climactic course, the automobilist drove drunk out of her mind causing a life-threatening accident. Rayan's limp body lay motionless without the appearance of life. Doris caused the death of a human being due to driving an automobile under the influence of alcohol. She launched Rayan's soul into eternity through vehicular homicide. While walking to Madea's house, the bearer of bad news imparted dismal information to Eve. Mr. Coleman expressed concern.

"Eve, how is the baby doing?"

"What do you mean, Mr. Coleman?" Eve asked while observing a fleet of police cars parked in front of Madea's house. Instinctively, Eve knew something happened. She ran screaming hysterically toward the accident. Madea caught her in a consoling grip.

"Eve, Rayan was hit by a car. He has a severe head injury. It does not look good. The severity of the injury appears fatal. Rayan's brain will be damaged."

"Oh! My baby is hurt!" Eve cried uncontrollably. She boarded the ambulance to the hospital. Mr. Edmonson, the funeral director, sent his son to Clover Street in order to clean the blood from the street.

"James, get up! Go to the Greene's house, now. They are friends of our family. I want you to clean that blood up left from the accident. They don't need to see the sight of blood."

"Okay daddy! I'll take a bucket of water."

"Take these sponges and rags." Mr. Edmondson instructed. All hell broke out again when Doris's sister visited Madea's house. The despicable demon confronted the family about the accident.

"My sister has been arrested for running over Eve's son. That baby didn't have any business with his ass in the street." Betty stated in an unkind mode.

"You are a cruel bitch. You are heartless heifer! You're a hardhearted specimen of a human being. How can you have the nerve to come to our house during our bereavement?" Lily said chastising the villain. Betty provoked Eve's sister, and Lily was ready to fight. Big Daddy prevented Lily form a bellicose battle. He demanded that the pugnacious pig vacate his property immediately. Mr. Edmondson was a dutiful funeral director. He helped the Greene family in several capacities. Once the insurance check was dispensed, he drove Eve to the lawyer's office. Upon asking for the insurance settlement, the lawyer informed Eve that her husband collected the check.

"Mr. Mimmus received the check early this morning," the attorney stated.

"I had no idea that he got the insurance check," Eve said shocked. "I need to pay Mr. Edmondson for my baby's funeral.

Supremacy Funeral Services has charge of the burial arrangements. I thank God for Mr. Anderson because he updated my child's policy," Eve said appreciatively. "If the insurance policy had lapsed because of non-payment, we could not afford to pay for his funeral." Newton emerged home later that night with $1,500.00 dollars left from the insurance money. Eve was astounded at the meager amount of money left from the insurance check. Newton squandered about a thousand dollars of their child's insurance money. The funeral ritual revealed how the baby succumbed to death making the supreme sacrifice. Rayan's young life reclined in the coffin devoid of life as through death. His soul traveled to one's final resting place. Eve's mind entered into a melancholy mood after the death of her baby. Suffering from melancholia, Eve moped around the house grief-stricken while morning the death of her child. Her academic focus dwindled from lack of concentration. She neglected the course of study for Elementary Education majors at LeMoyne-Owen College. Realizing that she could not centralize her mind on classes, Eve paid a trip to the Registrar's Office in order to drop the full load of courses required for the Spring Semester. She was academically astute, and her high grade-point average reflected successful accomplishments. The act of withdrawing from the college was recognized by President Hollis F. Price. He coerced Eve to stay in school.

"Hello! May I speak with Eve Mimmus, please?"

"This is Eve speaking." She said acknowledging the phone call.

"This is President Hollis Price. The Registrar made me aware of your withdrawal request. We need talented students enrolled in LeMoyne. I was informed about the loss of your son."

"Yes sir! I worry so much about my baby. It hurts deeply when one loses a child."

"I understand Eve, and you have my deepest condolences. We are concerned about your withdrawal from school. If you stay home, you will become more despondent about your baby's death. You need to keep yourself in school in order to focus mentally on the special tasks. Please come back to school."

"I missed my Professors' lectures. My analytical ability isn't suited to grasping knowledge in the academic world without my class notes."

"I will assign two students from your neighborhood to work with you. What course notes do you need?"

"I need the science and math notes."

"Judy is a math major, and Victoria is a science major. They live in Orange Mound. I will assign them to help you keep abreast of your class assignments."

"I know them, President Price. I appreciate your help. Thank you!" Eve was grateful for the encouragement. She burned the mid-night oil in preparation for her science and math test. The Physical Education exam was administered on Tuesday, but Eve had withdrawn from school the week before exams. She asked the Physical Education instructor for permission to take her exam. She knew the professor from the Mound because her parents owned

Supremacy Funeral Services in the neighborhood. Eve didn't expect preferential treatment, but she expected Ms. Edmondson to be cooperative. Sitting around the pool with her Hot Pants tightly fitting her buttocks, Ms. Edmondson entertained several young men.

"Excuse me, Ms. Edmondson. I missed my exam. I dealt with the death of my son, and I was so distraught that I didn't appear on campus on the day of the test. May I take my exam?"

"Taking your exam is out of the question. You see that I'm busy entertaining these handsome young men." She shrugged Eve off while flirting with the male students. "I refuse to waste my time observing you taking a test. I have better things to do." The Physical Education instructor stated with disdain. All the little boys hung around the bitch like hungry dogs. Ms. Edmondson provoked disgust in Eve's demeanor. Eve's outward behavior sought advice from the only Administrator at LeMoyne-Owen College who would understand her plight. Eve walked into President Hollis F. Price's office occupying a seat at his desk. Prying into the nature of the disagreement concerning the Physical Education final exam, President Price confronted Ms. Edmondson.

"Hello! Ms. Edmondson, this is President Price. I'm calling in reference to Eve Mimmus. She missed her Physical Education exam, and I have approved for her to take the necessary exams required for Eve to pass this Semester. If you don't have time to administer her exam, you may send the Physical Education exam to my office. I will give her the test myself."

"I can give her the test; I will be glad to administer the test," Ms. Edmondson said in a professional manner.

"I would prefer to give Eve the test in my office. Send a copy of the exam to me immediately."

"Yes sir! I will send one of my students to your office with the exam."

"Please don't forget to send the Key." He reminded her.

"I will send a copy of the Key." Ms. Edmondson said.

"Thank you, Ms. Edmondson." President Price stated courteously. Eve made exceptionally high scores on her final exams. As life evolved, Eve graduated from LeMoyne-Owen College. While her career began to excel, her marriage began to fail. Newton blazed the trail toward a northern compass point. He boarded the Greyhound Bus to New York City. Grandma Sally accompanied him to the bus station, and she took New Baby and Faith with her to bid him farewell. As the driver put the Greyhound in motion, Faith ran screaming behind the bus.

"Daddy! Oh Daddy! Don't leave me. Wait on me, daddy!" She chased the bus yelling for her father.

"Faith, come back here. Baby come back!" Grandma Sally yelled. "New Baby, run and catch her. Go get your sister." Grandma pleaded. Faith whooped at the top of her voice. She shed tears that turned on the waterworks. When all is said and done, Newton split the scene vanishing from his children's life. After settling in New York, Newton called Eve.

"Honey, I miss you. I messed up my family. I realize that I need you. We've been together since childhood. I've got a good job working at American Airlines. I want you and our children to move to New York. Will you move here?"

"I'm not moving to cold tail New York. If you mistreated me in Memphis, I don't know how you will react in New York. I will only move around the corner from my parents. I can depend on Big Daddy." Miles between Memphis and New York separated the couple. In due time, Eve filled for a divorce. The dissolution of the marriage bond ended in a legal confrontation. In the divorce decree, Eve sought custody of her children.

"Is Mr. Mimmus present with counsel?" The judge asked about Eve's husband.

"No, Your Honor! Mr. Mimmus resides in New York." Eve's attorney responded to the question. "Joint Physical Custody proposes a problem since the father does not live relatively close."

"The custody arrangement will become part of the divorce decree." The judge explained. "In my decree, I will name the parent with whom the children will live. At this juncture, these children are Wards of the Court. They are under the protection of the court. This court must decide which parent has the right to make decision for the children. I want the children to bear a charmed life." The judge accentuated.

"My client is petitioning the court for legal custody." The attorney called her desire to the attention of the judge.

"According to the legal relationship between a parent and her children, it is the right of the parent to provide shelter, medical care, and schooling for the offspring's. How can your client provide for these children?" The judge interrogated.

"Your Honor! My client is perfectly able to take care of her children. She is a college graduate, and she has signed a contract to teach for the Bluff City School System."

"Oh well! She is a college graduate with a job." The judge reiterated. "She can adequately provide for her children." The judge hit the gavel on his bench, and he said. "Divorce granted with custody of the children awarded to Mrs. Mimmus." Being self-sufficient, Eve provided for her children without social services. She did not receive Welfare or Child Support. Big Daddy and Madea helped with their grandchildren. Mr. Newton Mimmus Jr. had Cherokee Nation Supreme Court Chief Justice, would have deliberated in favor of Newton based upon nepotism. Since Judge Martin helped write the first Cherokee Constitution on July 26, 1827, his expertise could have written the divorce decree. Ironically, Newton III was born on July 26, 1947 of the same Cherokee lineage as Judge John Martin. Nevertheless, the bill of divorcement granted the parting of ways.

Chapter 3.

MRS. RATCHET

Ratchet is a terminology in an urban environment describing a woman who is out of control while dealing with dirty activities in the ghetto. Ratchet in the Urban Dictionary functions as an adjective describing the negative qualities of a lewd woman. She is whack. Webster does not define the term ratchet in relationship to a woman. In Webster, the vocabulary word is associated with a wheel. A ratchet person does not have any class; she has no finesse. This is Negro slang used in the hood. This lingo is indicative of the Non-Standard English used in the ghetto. While fraternizing in Harlem, Newton met Mrs. Ratchet. Her clear-sighted questing mind was aware of Newton's country boy image. He was from down South as northerners' described people. Newton lived with his older brother, Augustus, until a place of residence became available. He enjoyed socializing with Mrs. Ratchet. She showed Newton how to survive in a fast city. Mrs. Ratchet patronized establishments in the Melrose neighborhood in the New York borough of the Bronx on a regular basis. It was categorized as one of the poorest neighborhoods in America with heavy gang activities. Melrose was infested with drugs and prostitution. This borough was Mrs. Ratchet's old stumping ground, and she dawdled along the Track turning tricks. She used philandering along with her prostituting skills to intrigue Newton. She won his affection, and she became the light of his life. He was infatuated with her worldly ways. At that point, Newton lost his heart to a whore. After several months of courting, Mrs. Ratchet became pregnant. Being a man of honor, Newton married her. The couple tied the nuptial knot because they procreated a child. Using the baby as leverage, she trapped Newton in a marriage with sexual pit falls about paternity. Questions arose about the paternity of the first-born daughter because of her dark complexion. Newton's genealogy stemming from the Cherokee Indian tribe bestowed a light complexion skin tone on him with curly wavy hair. With both having a light complexion skin tone, Newton and Mrs. Ratchet produced a dark skin tone baby girl. In order to justify the little girl's unusual hereditary traits, they placed the blame on Newton's mother whose skin tone was a paper sack brown rather than black. However, the baby girl's skin tone was black as a skillet. Willie Lynch's color theory continues to dominate the mentality of some people. The light-skin verses dark-skin concept sets barriers on race relations within the Black community. The color of a person's skin determines not an individual's intellectual ability. People should not be judged by skin color. The color of one's skin does not define a person's character. When an individual is comfortable with one's identity, stereotypical labels do not affect a person's self-esteem. It does not matter if you are light-skin or dark-skin. With the birth of Verlie, the truth of paternity was the issue rather than the color of the baby's skin. Newton' attempt to make a whore into a housewife failed miserably. Woe is Newton! He took Mrs. Ratchet's hand for better or for worse, but marriage to her was for the worse. She had a five-year old daughter from a previous relationship. Now, she alleged that Newton fathered her unborn child. Newton and Mrs. Ratchet produced two more light-skin tone daughters. During the fullness of time, Eve was the source of her children's supply. However, she was a strict disciplinarian with an overprotective parental perception. While attending the University of Orange Mound, New Baby and Faith learned the language of the Hood. Duke Osborne taught them the first profane, foul-mouth four letter word which is functional in the ghetto. The Osborne children were a bunch of naughty little brats. Professor Duke introduced everyone on Clover Street to a new vocabulary word.

"I'm going to teach you-all a new word. I want yawl to say the pronouns 'she' and 'it' real fast." New Baby, Faith, Vickie, Bobby, and Beth uttered the pronouns several times while gliding the words into one syllable. Once the word was formulated, the word 'shit' was pronounced. Duke commanded Bobby to pronounce the new word for his mother. The Clover Street children marched into Bobby's house.

"Mommy, I learned a new word. I can say shit." He
enunciated proudly. Mrs. Simpson slapped Bobby upside the head
with a violent force.

"Don't use profanity. You should never use a curse
word." Everybody laughed, but the incident wasn't funny to
Bobby. In reality, he got slapped for not using profanity.
According to the etymology of the word 'shit', the acronym was
derived from the phrase Ship High in Transit. The phrase was
posted on ships transporting manure. A stable home environment
was created for Eve's children. She married an entrepreneur. The
couple purchased a house on Hampton Street near Deaderick
Avenue which was named in honor of the Deaderick Plantation.
Eve held steadfast to her vow of moving around the corner from
Big Daddy. She didn't venture far from the Mound. However, the
death angel flew Eve's husband's soul to a new plane. Faith
advanced in years from girlhood to adolescence. In high school,
she participated in the following extra-curricular activities: the
cheerleaders, the R.O.T.C, the Drama Club, and the Charming
Ladies Social Club. She even wore the royal crown of Ms.
Sophomore. On the contrary, Faith actively participated in teenage
antics. She mingled with Rena and Christy at Reverend Bolden's
house. Reverend Bolden was Christy's grandfather, but he never
spent time at home. To compensate for his lack of guidance, the
pastor bestowed plenty of money on Christy. Being a generous
soul, she spent money on Rena and Faith. Whenever they visited,
Christy took them to the Harlem House for Hot Dog Specials or

Hamburger Specials. Without adult supervision, the girls had the freedom to indulge in sinful infractions. Christy conducted Smoking Lessons for her friends.

"We are teenagers now. Eventually, we will be old enough to go to a club. We can party at the Hawaiian Isles. I'm going to teach you how to act in the club." At that moment, Christy poured her friends a glass of Pepsi Cola. "Imagine that this drink is an alcoholic beverage. We will drink whiskey. Take a sip." Then, Ms. Instructor lit a cigarette for each little vulnerable girl. "Puff on the cigarette. You will look older, and you will appear mature with a cigarette. Inhale and blow the smoke slowly out your mouth." Faith and Rena followed her instructions explicitly. "Good! Now, inhale the smoke. Take a sip of the Pepsi. Then, blow the smoke out after swallowing the Pepsi. Good! When you drink the liquor, puff on the cigarette." Christy approved of their ability to drink and smoke. "We are ready for the club." While walking home, Faith was confronted by Mrs. Gloria Hopson who lived on the corner of Hampton Street and Park Avenue.

"Faith, you are so fast. I don't know what your mother is going to do with you," Mrs. Gloria Hopson expressed her opinion.

"She will manage." Faith said assuring her of Eve's ability to control her. Before Faith could arrive home, Mrs. Hopson called Eve to expose her daughter's comment. One fine evening, Christy decided to pass the time of day at WDIA Radio Station. She delighted in the idea of dating a well-known Disc

Jockey. She called Faith and Rena to ride in her new red Mustang on a trip to the station. They were ecstatic about visiting the first radio station in America to feature African-Americans. Upon reaching her destination, Christy was totally ignored by the Disc Jockey. His regular female companion achieved recognition. Her father was an Award-Winning producer. Mitch Poindexter was an American soul and R & B record Producer in Memphis, Tennessee.

"Who are you?" Christy asked.

"I'm Karen Poindexter. My daddy is the famous Mitch Poindexter. He produces all the local singers and musicians in Memphis." Karen said. Christy and her clique parted from the radio station without acting a fool. However, the evening became full of foolery as the time wore on into later hours.

"Bubba Boyd is having a party. I know John is going to the party. I heard that he is dating Janice Stanford behind my back." Rena explained her romantic dilemma. "I want to crash the party."

"Madea told me never to go anywhere without an invitation." Faith advised.

"I am going to that party." Rena stated with conviction. "Christy drive over to Bubba's house. I want to see." Rena commanded. "I'm so pissed off. I don't know what to do." Rena walked eagerly to the front door knocking loudly. She and Christy entered observing John slow dancing with Janice. While observing her lover embracing another woman, feelings aroused fury fuming thoughts that flustered Rena. She was upset. They devised a plan of action. Christy drove to the grocery store, and she purchased the following items: a carton of eggs and several tomatoes. As a form of revenge, the young ladies threw eggs and tomatoes on several cars parked at the party. Christy parked her red Mustang at the Telephone Booth in front of the Sundry Store on the corner of Pendleton and Deaderick in the Mound. They covertly called the Memphis Fire Department, and they reported a fire burning at Bubba's residence. While watching the fire truck en route to the house, the girls were inflamed with wrath. While Faith helped Christy and Rena solve their romantic problems, she should have swept around her own front door. She should've solved her own romantic triangle with Ronald. Ronnie was a known gangster and womanizer. After watching the episode, they put in an appearance at Christy's house again. Reverend Bolden was sleeping soundly. So, the girls sat on the front porch discussing the various incidents. The dawn of daybreak burst through the sunrise introducing the early morning hours. Faith arrived home at 5:00 A.M. in the morning. Eve was highly perturbed. She was steamed up with anger.

"You stayed away from home all night. You cannot come home at any time of the morning. You can't walk in my house at 5:00 A.M. in the morning. You are only sixteen years old. You are not going to disrespect my house, and you are not going to disrespect yourself. I'm calling your father. I'm sending you to New York." Eve dialed the long-distance number to New York.

Faith stood silent dreading the idea of moving to New York. Faith didn't want to live in New York. She was perfectly satisfied living in Memphis.

"Newton, this is Eve. Your daughter came home at 5:00 A.M. this morning. In fact, she just walked in the house. She had the audacity to walk in here after staying out all night. Newton, you need to talk to her."

"Put her on the phone, please. Eve, thanks for calling to let me know about her actions."

"Hello!" Faith answered in a humble mood.

"Sugar, your mother told me that you stayed away from home all night." Newton referred to Faith using the endearing name bestowed upon her by the fatherly figure. He always called her Sugar. Newton revealed his paternal protective style. "Sugar, a man does not respect a woman who stays out late."

"Daddy, I wasn't with a man." Faith attempted to explain, but Newton needed to impart words of wisdom to his daughter.

"Don't allow him to keep you out during the wee hours in the morning. Sugar, don't lose your self-respect. I will be calling to check on you." He warned. Years later, Newton flew to Memphis with his new family. The father paved a way to make the acquaintance of his children. Faith was nineteen years old, and New Baby was twenty-one years old. The siblings in Newton's clan were introduced to their little sisters. Mrs. Ratchet's oldest daughter by a previous relationship did not make the trip to Memphis. However, Newton's biological daughters came. His first-born daughter by Mrs. Ratchet was ten years old; the second born daughter was nine years old, and the last daughter was six years old. Newton called Faith to arrange for the children to come into contact with each other.

"Hello Sugar! I'm in Memphis. I'd like to see you and New Baby."

"New Baby is at work. I'll let him know that you're in town." Faith informed their father about her brother's employment status.

"I'm staying with Jordan and Anita Hickman on Baltimore Street. I want you to meet my wife and daughters."

"Okay! I have a class at 9:00 A.M. today. I'll come to visit when I leave LeMoyne-Owen. I'm taking 12 hours in college this semester."

"That's great, Sugar. I'll see you soon." Newton said anticipating spending quality time with his daughter. Upon arriving at Mr. and Mrs. Hickman's, Faith parked her red Volkswagen. She was proud of her vehicle. Faith stopped college for a semester, and she worked on the Assembly Line at Holiday Press. Working the night-shift, she saved money from every pay check. She purchased the Volkswagen for transportation purposes. After Faith decided to continue her education, Eve inherited the Volkswagen car note. Now, Faith could travel to any destination. The Volkswagen traveled many miles with her cousin Tim. He was her cater-cousin: a close friend. Eve and her sister, Lily, were pregnant during the same time. Hence, Tim and Faith were six months apart. Therefore, Tim played the role of best friend in Faith's life. Riding from Orange Mound to Raleigh Springs Mall, Tim showed her how to down shift the Volkswagen. They enjoyed spending time together when Tim came home for breaks from Harvard University. During those times, he taught Faith to play Chess.

"Check Mate", he said while capturing her King. "Never let anyone Fool Mate you." He warned.

"What is Fool Mate?" She asked.

"Fool Mate occurs when a person captures your King in three moves." He informed her. Now, the little red Volkswagen Bug navigated to visit Faith's father. Faith's preordained encounter with her father presented paternity bonds from birth.

"Hello Daddy!"

"Hello Sugar! I'm glad to see you." Newton said while hugging his daughter. "This is my wife, Martha."

"It's nice meeting you, Martha." Faith said welcoming the introduction.

"It's nice meeting you, too. I like your outfit. It is real pretty." Mrs. Martha Ratchet complimented Faith's clothes. "Your father won't buy me any clothes," Mrs. Ratchet said complaining.

"You need to buy yourself some clothes like my mother. She works, and she buys clothes for all of us." Faith said advising her step-mother. However, Mrs. Ratchet did not take Faith's advice. She continued to neglect the duties of a good mother. She loved the streets. She acted in a dysfunctional manner by leaving her children home alone during the night hours while Newton worked the night shift for American Airlines at LaGuardia Airport. Mrs. Ratchet sneaked away from the apartment immediately after Newton left for work. She patronized a neighborhood plagued by high levels of drug use and prostitution. Mrs. Ratchet abandoned her daughters for a lifestyle of indulging with the vices in society on Melrose. Each daughter expressed an opinion concerning the lack of motherly duties by Mrs. Ratchet. The daughters discussed the deplorable maternal ability of their mother. They decided to vote their mother out. Their election choice voted to dismiss Mrs. Ratchet out the house. Newton was a Man above all men. Left with the responsibility of raising three daughters, Newton became Mr. Mom. Mrs. Ratchet neglected her oldest daughter. Carol remained with Mrs. Ratchet during the separation because she was not Newton's biological child. Mrs. Ratchet wanted to do her own thing. Her thing was snorting Coke. Mrs. Ratchet was hooked on Cocaine. Carol was destined to live in a drug infested home environment. Lines of Coke was a permanent fixture on their Living Room table. Mrs. Ratchet only cared about drugs: not her daughters. Don was her drug dealer. He constantly supplied her with Caine. Don came to visit Mrs. Ratchet's apartment, but he was not alone. Like a trailing cloud of dust, five of his friends strolled in behind him. Mrs. Ratchets place was the Party Pad. Don kept her high. He served her with a snowy white powder that ruined her life. Carol had to contend with a lot of traffic coming through the house. People visited the drug house to snort Coke or hit the pipe. Don was a big shot. At this moment, he was the man of the house. Don and his comrades were drinking beer, smoking marijuana, and snorting Cocaine. They had the music turned up to its maximum level. Carol had not dozed off to sleep. Lying in bed, she heard everything. She lived in a dwelling of discontentment. Holy havoc broke out in her room. The peace and serenity that she experienced was interrupted by Don. The pervert creeped into her bedroom. He walked over to Carol's bed.

"Hi Sweetie! You're Martha's cute daughter. I like you. I got bored down stairs," he explained. "Were you sleeping?" He sat on the foot of her bed.

"Hi Mr. Don. I was trying to sleep."

"Well, you can stay up a little later tonight. I will keep you company." As they talked at length, his hand suddenly stroked her hair. His hand moved aggressively toward her breast.

"What are you doing?" She asked in astonishment. "Don't put your hands on me," she demanded.

"Shut up, bitch! You need to experience a man. I know what to do with a sweet young thang like you. I'm going to have sex with you. I'm gonna fuck you good." Don bragged.

"You can't do nothing with me," she informed him. "Do it with momma."

"I'd rather do it with you." His hand moved toward her again. Instinctively, she moved to another spot on the bed.

"Leave me alone," Carol pleaded. "I've never had sex in my life."

"You what?" Amazement filled his face. "Great! Your hymen hasn't been broken. That's one membrane I want to break." Carol shivered with fear. She didn't want him to break anything on he. Carol had never heard of a hymen.

"What's a hymen?" She asked

"It is a little membrane going across your pussy." Suddenly, he placed hi hand between Carol's legs and touched her vagina. She knocked his hand away. Carol detested Don's hands going anywhere near her. Don's devious mind began to clock. His mind ticked in the wrong direction. Mischievous thoughts conjured up cruel deeds to be performed. He covered Carol's mouth to keep her from screaming. It was like a bad dream. She experienced a volatile incident with Don violating her body. Placing a lubricant between the young tikes' legs, Don prepared her vagina for the carnal sin. This was a night of doom and gloom. He sexually molested Carol. The criminal entered her pussy violating the child's virginity. Inserting his penis into her virgin vagina, he punctured Carol's hymen. It was taboo to sexually abuse a child. A child molestation act could only be performed by a queer.

"I hate you!" Carol screamed. "Look at this blood dripping from me! You hurt me. This creamy white liquid gushing from my vagina is flowing down my legs." The slings and arrows of her word condemned Don.

"I love that good tight pussy you've got. Damn! It was good." The essence of life had been filled with serenity until Carol's mother sold her for Cocaine. Carol's blissful life was disturbed by a child molester. She whooped and hollowed until the wee-wee hours in the morning. Carol finally drifted off to sleep. The next day, she was disoriented. Carol stumbled out of bed the next morning heartbroken. The sexual act was very familiar to her mind. Carol questioned her identity. She wondered what was wrong with her. She undertook a quest to find the person hidden deep inside. Seeking to search deep within, she had yet to find Carol. Her thoughts were pure as water, but her body showed signs of impurity. A stranger stole her soul by invading her body reaching his main goal. All the laughter, joy, and gladness had been wiped away from her face. The memories of yesterday wouldn't go away. She whined sitting in the chair at school. The teacher observed Carol's restless, crying spirit.

"Carol, What's wrong? You've been crying all morning. You're not concentrating on your assignment. Talk to me, darling."

"I've got a problem, Ms. Brooks. I need to talk with you privately."

"We need to contact the Guidance Office." Ms. Brooks pushed the Intercom button to call the school's office.

INTERCUT – INTERCOM SYSTEM

"Office! May I help you?" The secretary answered.

"This is Ms. Brooks. I have a sick student. I need to take her to the Guidance Office."

"I will send a Teacher's Assistant to monitor your class." The secretary said.

"Thank you!" Ms. Brook said graciously. The Guidance Counselor questioned Carol extensively about her problem.

"Carol! Ms. Brooks is concerned about you. Your teacher said that you are hurting. Where are you hurting?"

"I'm hurting down here. He hurt my hymen thing." Carol revealed.

"Who harmed your hymen?"

"Don hurt me. He had sex with me."

"Who is Don?"

"He is my momma's friend. He forced me to have sex with him. He put that thing in me, and it hurt so bad." Carol explained.

"Carol, that is non-consensual sexual rape. Sexual touching of a child is a Crime. The laws protect children from criminal acts of sexual abuse." The Guidance Counselor uncovered the laws pertaining to child abuse.

"We must make a report to the authorities immediately." Ms. Brooks stated. "As a school employee, we are bound by law to report this sexual violation."

"You're right," the Guidance Counselor agreed. The legal codes state that professionals must report incidents when we suspect child abuse. I'll contact the police. In the meantime, we

need to take Carol to the Children's Hospital to be examined."
The doctor placed Carol on the examination table. The diagnoses
revealed the puncturing of her vagina.

"This child has undergone sexual abuse." The doctor
informed the school personnel.

"Carol! A police officer must be given a sworn statement
about the charges given by you. The police were dispatched to the
hospital to write a report.

"Young lady! I'm Detective Flanagan. I need to ask you
some questions. We need to apprehend the person who hurt you.
Who did this to you, Carol?"

"His name is Don." I said.

"We will make sure that Don doesn't hurt you again." The
officer pledged to protect Carol. "We're going to place you at
Juvenile tonight until we find you a nice Foster home."

"I need to call momma to let her know where I am."

"The Department of Human Services will contact your
mother." The officer reassured her. When the counselor from
Human Services arrived, she explained the policies of the agency.

"We can't let you go back into that home environment,"
stated Ms. Roberts. "We're going to take you to Juvenile Hall.
You will be safe there. We will have to prosecute Don. He should
serve time in jail for his crime. Carol adjusted well to life in
Juvenile Hall. She met many girls whose life's experiences were
similar to hers. She was not alone. They shared a common bond:
child abuse. Two days later, Don was arrested and charged with

child sexual abuse. An eerie feeling permeated throughout my body as we walked into the court room. This was the day of the Preliminary trial. The bailiff stood in front of the court room dressed in an olive-green uniform with emblems and a shiny gold badge adorning the outfit. When the judge walked into the Chamber, the bailiff instructed everyone to rise. The court clerk introduced the case. He said with a husky voice,

"The People vs. Donald Taylor. The indictment number is 473-77." The state furnished Carol with an attorney. Don hired his own lawyer. He faced a long prison sentence for child molestation. Don could get a minimum period of imprisonment of 25 years for the rape of a child. Carol's testimony was strengthened by the presentation of the examining physician. The medical exam offered a semen analysis as factual evidence. Carol's attorney sought to use any successful legal maneuver. A Class A Felony would get Don 15-62 years in prison. The case was based on the sworn statement of a child. Attorney McMillan began to delve into the case. He cited the court case known as the People vs. Brash as a foundation for her case. The lawyer spoke about the court's power.

Defense Attorney:	A conviction cannot be handed down based on a child's testimony.
Prosecutor:	If the child's testimony is corroborated, a criminal conviction will be the Judgment.
Defense Attorney:	The case has to be strengthened by

evidence.

Prosecutor:	The medical examination will confirm the act of rape. As the public Prosecutor, I may decide to indict the case based on the medical examination.

This gave Don a sense of hopelessness. Our attorney began to delve into the case. Because Don stood steadfast to his innocence, the lawyer mentioned Corpus Delicti as a possible defense. The facts revealed the commission of a sex offense.

The Prosecutor called Carol to the witness stand.

Prosecutor:	Did your mother have any visitors the night of the alleged rape?
Witness:	Yeah!
Prosecutor:	How many people were present?
Witness:	Five of Don's friends were there.
Prosecutor:	Were there any other ladies at your house that night?
Witness:	No sir!
Prosecutor:	Did your mother entertain men often?
Witness:	Yes!
Prosecutor:	Did they party at your house on weekends?
Witness:	They gathered at our apartment every day.
Prosecutor:	Did they drink a lot of alcohol and use drugs?

Witness:	Both! They drank booze and smoked
Witness:	Caine. They even smoked marijuana.
Prosecutor:	Is the rapist present in this court room?
Witness:	Yes sir! He is sitting over there."
Prosecutor:	Your next witness.
Defense Counsel:	With such a heavy traffic flow in your house, any one of those men could have raped you.
Prosecutor:	Objection! He is leading the witness.
Judge:	Sustain!
Defense Counsel:	You may step down,

A surprise twist of the tale was introduced by the Defense Counsel. The defense walked slowly over to Don. Don whispered something in his ear.

Defense Counsel:	If it pleases the court, the defendant has a request. Donald Taylor solicits permission to withdraw his plea. He previously entered a not guilty plea. Thereupon, he desires to enter a plea of guilty to child molestation.
,Defendant:	Hurry up! I want to get this shit out of the way.
Judge:	Restrain your client. I will hold you in contempt.
Prosecutor:	Mr. Taylor, you need the advice of your attorney. Have you had ample time to

	discuss the circumstances of your plea?
Defendant:	I have.
Prosecutor:	Is it true that you desire to withdraw your plea of not guilty to the indictment charging you with child sexual molestation?
Defendant:	Yeah!
Prosecutor:	With this plea, Mr. Taylor, you waive Your right to a trial by jury upon the Indictment. Do you waive that right?
Defendant:	I do.
Prosecutor:	Has anyone in the legal field persuaded you through threats to change your plea?
Defendant:	No sir!
Clerk:	The court will approve your plea of guilty to the lesser offense of child molestation in the first degree.

Donald Taylor was convicted on the charges, and he received a 10-year sentence.

Chapter 4.

DECEIT

On March 29, 1879, some British and Colonial troops under the Command of Colonel Henry Evelyn Wood called a major attack by the African Zulu tribesmen. On the American home-front, African-Americans in the Orange Mound community sought economic stability. In 1879, former slaves sought personal spiritualism and the start of a life of freedom. Hence, Mt. Malachi organized as a religious institution in Orange Mound in 1879. Big Daddy and Madea joined Mt. Malachi C.M.E. Church in the heart of the Mound on Park Avenue. The organized religious body united human beings in a relationship with a superior being. The spiritual-minded people gathered in the house of worship. The Exodus to Orange Mound after the Civil War fostered pride in the mind-set of the people. Eve and her siblings were taught ethical values. In accordance with the accepted standards of conduct, they followed a code of ethics. They learned the lessons of life based upon morality. The fundamental truth about praising God with the enemy instilled religious rules of conduct in Eve. Edna Bee and her two sisters were members at Mt. Malachi. They used the bully technique to intimidate Eve on Sunday. The sisters taunted her, but Eve practiced the art of ignoring fools. An ignoramus continued to hold on to a defunct romantic relationship; Edna Bee couldn't let go. Newton terminated the love affair with her, and he moved to New York City. Since Edna Bee's sister lived next door to the church, Eve came in contact with them on Sunday mornings. She decided to ignore them.

"I'm not speaking to her. She ruined my marriage." Eve expressed disdain for Edna Bee.

"You might as well speak." Faith said. "She didn't get him, and you don't need him." From the mouth of a babe, words of wisdom were expressed. Eve perceived the true nature of forgiveness from her child.

"You are right." Eve agreed. They spoke friendly to the sisters, and the ladies spoke pleasantly. Families were interconnected in Orange Mound. Generations of kinfolks grew-up in this neighborhood, and the family legacy was handed down from generation to generation. Eve contend with contempt from several enemies at Mt. Malachi CME Church. Hannah and Francis Billingston continued to stir the tide of animosity against her. The spirit manifestation of malice showed, and Hannah's crush on Newton lingered in her heart since childhood. The sisters were evil personified. The young ladies emphasized a sense of rivalry. They hung Eve spiritually for public scorn. Eve's daughter, Faith, was their primary target. While living on the Deaderick Planation in Orange Mound, the Willie Lynch Syndrome was used to control Black folks. In 1712, Willie Lynch implemented a method for controlling Black slaves. He outlined a number of differences among Black people. Willie Lynch maintained that instilling envy controls the minds of Black people. He ascertained that envy embedded in the mental thought patterns of niggers would be stronger than adulation, respect, or admiration. The envy harbored within Hannah and Francis' heart pierced Eve's life in many ways. Mentally, Blacks condemn each other based on the Willie Lynch theory of Color. Colorism and classism are customary in the African-American community. Mrs. Hannah Billingston attacked Faith with the Willie Lynch doctrine of Color on Sunday at church.

"Good morning! Come and sit in my car with me. We are early for Sunday service." Hannah invited Faith to socialize with her before services. "You are a nice-looking young lady. You are light-skinned, and you've got fine wavy hair. Those qualities have advantages and disadvantages." Willie Lynch's color method differentiated between light-skinned blacks and dark-skinned blacks. Hannah utilized the indoctrination of the Willie Lynch theory to control Faith's destiny with her negative thoughts. On the plantation, light-skinned Blacks worked in the Master's mansion while dark-skinned Blacks worked in the hot fields. Hannah gave birth to one medium brown-skinned daughter and one dark-skinned daughter. She taught for Bluff City Schools, and her husband opened his own Law Firm. However, the rumor mill revealed that the dark-skin daughter was conceived by a well-known construction company entrepreneur. Francis Billingston's daughter, Nancy, became chummy with Faith while worshipping at

Mt. Malachi CME Church. A deceptive relationship existed between Nancy and Faith. They mingled at social affairs, and Nancy invited Faith to a party welcoming her cousin Dianne Billingston from Colorado. Faith admired her pierced ears at sixteen years old, and Dianne pierced Faith's ears in Hannah Billingston's kitchen during the party. While worshipping at church, Nancy and Faith engaged in conversations on a regular basis. Nancy preached about her cousin's attributes instead of listening to the Preacher. Nancy conversed in depth about her handsome cousin from Jackson, Mississippi. He was the topic of conversation for years. Faith listened attentively, and she desired to fall in love with her cousin. Faith was in the market for a new love since her high school sweetheart died at an early age after living a life of crime in Orange Mound. Faith realized the importance of selecting a mate with good qualities. She visualized with the power to picture mentally a love affair with Butch Billingston. Faith's creative use of pictorializing created fancy romantic figments of love in her imagination. After graduating from Wildcat's Den High School, Faith enrolled in Jackson State University. Faith requested the presence of Butch Billingston when she arrived on the Jackson State campus.

"I want to meet Butch Billingston. Do you know him?" Faith asked Jimmy Anderson. She was in Jimmy's class, and they enjoyed discussing the assignments.

"Yeah! I know him. We are from Jackson. We grew up in Jack Town."

"Will you tell him Faith Mimmus wants to meet him?"

"Sure! He is in the Campus Recreation Center. I'll tell him now."

A few minutes later, a tall handsome young man greeted Faith.

"Hi! Are you Faith? I'm Butch. Jimmy told me that you wanted to meet me."

"Yes! I'm from Memphis, and I heard about you from your cousin Nancy." They sat under the big Oak Tree shooting the breeze for hours. After the initial meeting, they were a couple for years. The love affair was true to life: true to reality. When she became a sophomore, Butch became a Senior. She wrote the following message in his annual:

Reserved for Faith Mimmus

Dear Sir,

After one year and eight months of Extensive Research, I am pleased to announce my most affectionate feelings for you and to wish you success in all your endeavors. I, Faith Mimmus a victim of true love, would like to wish you all the success and happiness in the world. I wish you success; however, I would like to be by your side and work along with you in order to reach our goal. A goal that might seem excrescent or superfluous, but nevertheless, it is a necessary one. There are times, Butch, when this goal may seem impossible. It may appear to be a form of Platonic idealism. Yet when this goal is reached, we will witness a form of materialistic philosophy together. I feel that we have a beautiful relationship even though at times it sets its pace upon the verge of destruction At these difficult times, we seem to overcome that deathly fate which will divide us forever. Butch, I want you to know that I am proud of you. I am proud because you have made the step to the future, and I am proud because you are mine: all mine. I'll always love you, Butch: for better or for worse. If God choose, I shall love thee better after death.

With Loads of Love,

Faith Mimmus

Ironically, Eve's daughter's romantic relationship with a Billingston staged Situational Irony in the interaction of family ties. The Shakespearn type feud between the Billingston's and Greene's caused a bone of dissension in the union of Butch and Faith. While in the Dormitory, Kaleigh told Faith important information concerning Butch's paternity of an offspring by Angela Wright.

"Did you know that Butch has a baby by Angela Wright?"

"No, I didn't know. I'm going to call him, now. I want to hear his version about fatherhood." Faith entered the phone booth on her Dormitory's hall. After the phone rang about five times, Butch answered.

"Hello Butch, I have an important question for you. Do you have a baby by Angela Wright? A young lady in the Dorm told me about the baby." Faith explained in search of an answer.

"No! Angela's baby is not mine. That is Lawrence's baby. Lawrence is my best friend, and I met her while hanging around Lawrence's apartment. She is Lawrence's girlfriend. They dated for years. Lawrence has kept an apartment since his father died. His father worked for Bluff City Light Gas and Water, but he was electrocuted while working on the job. After his mother's demise, Lawrence became self-sufficient. He continued to attend Jackson State University, and he worked a part-time job. Angela spent many romantic hours at Lawrence's apartment." Butch explained the situation with Angela Wright.

"If that is your baby, I need to know. You need to be a father to the baby. I know what life is like to grow up without a father. I can move on with a new guy," Faith compromised.

"That's not my baby. She was dating Lawrence. Angela was his lady." Butch confirmed. "Lawrence and Angela ended their relationship for about a month. I thought they got their romantic relationship back together." Butch revealed. "Lawrence and I have been friends since high school." Butch reminisced about their fun-times in Jack Town. "Lawrence is dating your friend Laura, now." Lawrence and Laura were a couple, and Faith formed a close friendship with them because of Butch. Faith and Laura developed a bond of sisterhood, and they became the best of friends.

"I enjoy our friendly relationship with Lawrence and Laura," Faith revealed her loyal friendship.

"Yes, they are cool people." Butch admitted. "Let's go to the Recreation Center. Would you like anything to eat?"

"I want a Hamburger and a Soda."

"You've got it." Butch said. In search of privacy, Butch and Faith found a secluded place on campus to court. Angela stalked them in the Administration Building. Upon seeing the couple, Angela didn't make a wry face. She maintained a pleasant disposition. At a later time, a visit from the Stork delivered a beautiful baby girl to Angela. Angela sought emotional refuge with Lawrence. She cheated on Lawrence by having an affair with Butch, but he gave her a listening ear.

"Hi Lawrence! I haven't seen you in a long time." Angela greeted her ex-boyfriend.

"Yes, I haven't seen you since last semester. How is your pretty little daughter?" Lawrence asked.

"She's growing so fast." Angela said with a smile. "I love her so much. When I see Butch, he doesn't speak to me." Angela said seeking sympathy from the very guy deceived by her affair with Butch. Butch received sexual benefits from Angela at Lawrence's expense.

"That's what you get out of life." Lawrence pointed out life's consequences to Angela. Butch and Faith enjoyed riding around Jack Town.

"Laura and I are going to Memphis this weekend. I'm going to enjoy having my best friend around the house with the family. We always have a good time." Faith disclosed her weekend plans to Butch. Faith looked forward to partying with Laura in the Bluff City.

"I'll see you upon my arrival to campus." Butch vowed to see Faith after her visit home. Faith returned to the Dormitory. She walked down the hall to her friend Laura's room. They made plans for the weekend. For entertainment, New Baby made plans to amuse his sister and her friend. New Baby matured from a boy to a Man. As a rite of passage, the guys in the Mound bestowed the name Man upon New Baby. In the hood, Man was pronounced with a macron over the letter /a/ revealing a pronunciation of the word /main/. Man was a southern gentleman born in the ghettos of Orange Mound. On the rise to adulthood, this gentleman travelled life in the fast lane. New Baby's ventures unveiled another chapter in life. To entertain his sister and Laura, Man planned to take them to a Night Club. They were determined to make a night of it. The gibber-jabber in the car kept the merrymaking exciting. The traffic on Parkway was busy as usual with the screeching of brakes and tires while the roaring of heavy traffic moved vehicles speedily in South Memphis. Reggie was the designated driver in his Cadillac. Man met Reggie while working for Big Tony Caraceni as Drug Runners. Reggie flirted with Faith, but Man objected to his flirtatious move on his sister. In the final analysis, Man didn't want his sister dating a guy of his infamous character. The garrulous expression of friendship allowed the group to enjoy the friendly association for the night. Man introduced the girls to marijuana.

"Let's smoke some weed. I've got a joint," Man suggested.

"What's a joint?" Faith asked.

"It is an herb. Herbs are made from plants." Man revealed his horticulture knowledge. "You smoke marijuana in the form of a cigarette, but you hold the smoke inside when inhaled." The young ladies plastered their minds with marijuana. Their endorphins were polluted. Faith and Laura were high in spirits while feeling high as a kite. The girls' minds were flushed in a dopey frame of mind. Marijuana gave them a euphoric feeling. Reggie offered Faith and Laura a Christmas Tree pill that narcotizes the victim. Christmas Trees were pills with red and green strips.

"Sis! Don't take that pill. It is a psychedelic. The Christmas Tree is a hallucinogenic. Don't be a dope fiend. Sis! Don't fuck with it." Man cautioned. Tomfoolery didn't make a fool out of Faith and Laura. Faith completed the Spring Semester, and she withdrew from Jackson State University. Eve was highly perturbed when Faith withdrew from school.

I am upset because you left Jackson State. I wanted you to get a college degree. What are you going to do in life?"

"I want a job." Faith confessed. "I'll find a job somewhere." She found a job on the Assembly Line packing brochures for the Holiday Inn Hotels. Faith formed a congenial relationship with her Assembly Line co-worker. During the break, Rita cordially communicated with her.

"Have you ever dealt with a White girl?" Rita asked while breaking the racial barrier.

"No," Faith admitted. "I've never dealt with a White girl. I grew up in Orange Mound. The Mound is a Black neighborhood." Faith explained.

"I'm your first White girlfriend." Rita pledged her unbiased friendship to Faith.

"Yes, you are my first White girlfriend. I'm proud to have a White girlfriend. I enjoy working with you, Rita." They resumed working, and they solidified the friendship. Eve complained about Faith's employment status to Madea.

"Madea, I wish Faith had stayed in school. I'm just dumfounded by her lackadaisical attitude about the acquisition of knowledge. I am glad that she bought a car, but I wish she had remained in school."

"Don't worry about her. She will come to a rude awakening eventually. She calls Big Daddy every day. They talk for hours until she falls asleep," Madea revealed her granddaughter's daily activities. Faith worked for Holiday Press for eight months; she realized the importance of an education. Faith resigned her position, and she enrolled in LeMoyne-Owen College to resume her education. However, her enduring friendship with Rita lingered in her heart for a life time. With a flashback to the earlier romantic relationship formed at Jackson State, Faith remained a prisoner of love. The Star-Cross lovers continued their romantic relationship after she moved back to Memphis. Butch drove to the Bluff City every weekend to enjoy a rendezvous with her. Butch had an innate connection to Memphis.

The family pedigree from his mother's descendants lived in South Memphis. Mum Maggie married his father after attending Jackson State University. The Billingston's had a family gathering during the Christmas Holiday season. Francis and Hannah drove to Jackson in order to enjoy the family festivities. Nancy brought her best friend. They had an ulterior motive for bringing Brenda. Nancy's aim was to undermine Faith's relationship with Butch. They planned to sway Butch's affection away from Faith. Mrs. Francis Billingston directed Butch's attention to Brenda.

"Butch, this is Brenda. She is the lady for you. You should be with her. Brenda has a Master's Degree from the University of Memphis."

"Hi!" Butch greeted the intruder while Faith stood silently next to him. The deceitful demons attempted to sabotage Faith's love affair with Butch.

"Sweetheart! Butch said addressing Faith. "Here is your Christmas gift." She unwrapped the present, and a beautiful black tweed double-breast sweater was in the box.

"Thank you, honey!" Faith said appreciatively.

"I would love that sweater," Brenda said flirting with Butch while disrespecting Faith. Brenda proved to be a formidable adversary. Faith couldn't fathom kicking her ass in Butch's grandparent's house. She resigned to break bread with enemies. Grandpa Grand's reputation as a wealthy entrepreneur spread across the state of Mississippi. Grandpa Grand's birth occurred in the 1890's when the Afro-American League formed in Chicago.

The Afro-American League laid the foundation for the formation of the NAACP. For the moment, Grandpa Grand gathered the family members for a portrait. Faith stood next to the photographer as the pictorial representation of the family appeared on film.

"Stop" Grand raised his voice to halt the picture. "Come here!" He urged Faith to move close to him. "You are a member of this family. You belong in our family portrait." The portraiture of the Billingston family included Faith. She smiled as the picture featured the family members. Finally, Faith graduated from LeMoyne-Owen College with a Bachelor of Arts Degree. Since Dr. Willard saw potential in Faith, the professor encouraged the college to hire her as a tutor in the Learning Resource Center. Wedding bells rang for Faith. Approximately a week before the wedding, Faith confronted Mum Maggie eyeball to eyeball about the rumor of Angela's baby. To her surprise, she denied Angela's baby. She claimed to be unaware of the birth of the child. In June, the goddess Juno united Butch and Faith in holy matrimony seven years after their initial meeting. Angela Wright's daughter was seven years old at the time of the wedding. Angela was smart, attractive, and friendly. However, Butch did not want her. The divine daggers were drawn at Mt. Malachi CME Church. Angela's brother became an Associate Minister. His main ministry was to censure Faith in church. Willie Lynch hypothesized about the Black man verses the Black woman method of controlling Black folks. As a black man of God, Reverend Wright formed opposition against her in the church. The Wright family members condemned Eve and Faith. Reverend Wright raked her over the coals during his fiery sermons at Mt. Malachi CME Church. The newlyweds drove to Jack Town for a devotional system of worship. After church, Butch and Faith went to his grandparents' house. Butch lived with his grandparents while the six sisters lived with their mother. The elder Billingston's were elated to have their grandson living with them after the death of their only son. After dinner, Grandma Nana confided in Faith. She discussed candidly problems with extramarital relations involving Grandpa Grand and her son. In privacy, Grandma Nana spoke to Faith on a woman to woman basis.

"You need to know about the first wife of Butch's father. My son was married to another lady. Maggie began dating him, and his first marriage ended in divorce. She moved to Chicago." Grandma Nana imparted valuable family relationship information to Faith. The sea of adultery streamed infidelity into Grandma Nana's marriage. Grandpa Grand's illicit intercourse produced children by two different women. Grandma Nana admitted her aggressive move to save her marital state.

"My husband broke our marriage vows. His sexual affairs were a violation of our marriage bed. I ran those two women out of Jackson. I refused to allow them to break-up my marriage." Mrs. Fonda Billingston was aware of Grandpa Grand's love affairs because she rented rooms in her Transit House in Orange Mound for his sexual entertainment. Therefore, Hannah and Francis

Billingston knew all the offsprings' conceived by Grandpa Grands outside his marriage. Faith realize that some marriages surmount infidelity while some end in Divorce Court. Butch's baby sister, Camille, confronted Faith revealing her feelings about the marriage.

"I didn't want Butch to get married. He should remain single, and he should ride around Jack Town in his Mercedes Benz." Camilla stated her opinion. Faith thought silently to herself.

"Bitch! It ain't what you want. It's all about what Butch wants, and he wants me." Faith ignored his baby sister, and she walked off silently. The couple planned to attend a Business Banquet near Natchez Trace. The historical trace was the major pathway for the Choctaw, Chickasaw, and Natchez Indians. The path extended from Natchez, Mississippi to Nashville, Tennessee. Confidentially, Faith expressed the inside information about the trip with her co-worker. Mrs. Boland was a wise old lady with prudent ideas.

"My husband wants me to accompany him to a banquet in Natchez, Mississippi, but I'm afraid to ask Mrs. Gillard." Faith said.

"You should attend the Banquet. Ask Sandra to grant you time off from work. You need to show up; you must make an appearance. You should direct attention to yourself. The entrepreneurs in that business community need to see his wife." Mrs. Boland encouraged Faith to attend the festivities. The ceremonial dinner entertained the couple with a feast. The entrepreneurs fed them luxuriously. Upon leaving the Banquet Hall, Butch's sisters concocted a plan to introduce him to a businessman's daughters.

"Butch! This is Mr. Donaldson's daughter." Sherry introduced the young lady from Natchez to her brother. "Don't you like her?" She asked enticing Butch to another female.

"Look at her pretty car, Butch." Camita focused her brother's attention to the young lady's pretty sky-blue vehicle. The nervy spunky sisters interrupted the marriage alliance. Faith kept busy working in the Learning Resource Center. The educational environment on the LeMoyne-Owen College's campus allowed time for Faith to study for her Master's Degree at the University of Memphis. She had access to LeMoyne's library. Faith formed a friendly relationship with Doris Tucker while working in the Learning Resource Center. Doris was married to Benny Tucker. However, the rumormongers alleged that Benny fathered Hannah Billingston-Smith's dark-skinned daughter. Nevertheless, Doris never mentioned her marital saga with Benny. A legal dissolution of the marriage bond between Benny and Doris occurred on April 5, 1974. At the same time, Hannah's husband filed a bill of divorcement. She cross-filed, and a decree of divorce was granted. At an advance time, Benny and Hannah married revealing the validity of their infidelity. Faith's nuptial tie unraveled when Butch refused to drive her to work.

"Sweetheart, my car won't start. Will you take me to work?"

"No! I am picking up my cousin. Marcus is riding to Jack Town with me. We've got plans to party." Butch refused to offer help.

"You can easily take me to work. Marcus lives around the corner from LeMoyne."

"Come on! I'm in a hurry." Butch urged her to quickly get into the car. Riding down Poplar Avenue, Butch complained. "You should've called your brother. He can take you to work."

"My brother should not have to drive all the way from Orange Mound to Collierville to take me to work." Faith lost her femininity by using foul language. "Let me out this motherfucker. You don't have to take me a damn place." She blasted his ass with cuss words. Man took his sister to work.

"Sis! I'm there for you. Whenever you need me, I'll help."

"Bro, thank you for coming to get me to work. I appreciate you." Faith said speaking affectionately to her brother.

"Sis, you know that I will do anything for you. Always remember what momma said. She loves Billie Holiday's song. The philosophical lyrics of Billie Holiday's song, 'God Bless the Child with His Own', became engrained in our minds. Momma taught us to be productive. We were taught to receive God's blessings with thankfulness." Man reminded his sister. He knew he necessity of accumulating property and assets. Faith's mother arrived promptly to get her after work. Eve was a good provider. As a single parent, she managed to provide her children with the necessities of life. It was necessary for Faith to have a car. Therefore, Eve agreed to furnish her with a new vehicle. Since Eve taught school, she made arrangements to co-sign for Faith a car at the Teacher's Credit Union. When she drove the new car to Jackson, Butch's sisters were highly upset. They assumed that he purchased the new car for Faith. He defused their anger by explaining that he didn't buy the car. The handsome husband began double-dealing romantically. Butch was apt to lie and cheat. Patricia exposed Butch's unfaithfulness.

"Have you ever thought about marriage counseling?" Patricia asked in search of a solution to the downfall of Faith's marriage.

"No! I haven't thought about counseling. Why do you ask me about marriage counseling?" Faith questioned.

"I want your marriage to work. Butch is courting."

"Who is he dating."

"Rosalind is courting your husband. She is Sherry's friend."

"Sherry involves herself in all of Butch's love affairs." Faith complained.

"Sherry should take care of her own defunct love affair." Patricia revealed a problem within Sherry's love live.

"How did Sherry's love affair end?" Faith asked.

"He left her at the Altar. Sidney was married to Talena. Everybody at Jackson State knew that Sidney was married, and he fathered several children. Honey, Sherry wouldn't listen. She wanted him, and she was determined to marry Sidney. He loved Talena, and he was committed to his marriage. So, he left Sherry standing at the altar without marrying her. He was at home with his wife while the wedding guest waited for the marriage ceremony." Patricia was from Jack Town, and her father was married to Butch's mother. Nightfall arrived, and Patricia left. Moving toward her husband's side of the bed about 4:00 A.M., Faith felt an empty side of the King size bed. Butch did not come home. He stayed away from home all night. Faith called Grandma Nana's house to inquire about Butch's presence at her house.

"Mrs. Billingston, this is Faith. Butch didn't come home. Did he stay at your house?" Grandma Nana looked in Butch's old room, but he was not sleeping in the room.

"No, Faith. He is not here." Grandma Nana disclosed. In pursuit of disrupting wedding bliss, Rosalind shacked with Butch. They entered into a Common-law-Marriage. Butch smoked marijuana, and he experimented with other drugs. Rosalind indulged with drugs while impressing him. The drugs desensitized Butch's feelings about life. Butch had the money bag for the bank deposit for the family business. In a drug daze, he grabbed a stash of money from the bank deposit bag. He threw the cash in the air.

"Money ain't shit!" He yelled while the bills fell to the floor. "Money ain't shit!" He said while Rosalind scrambled on the floor picking up all of the money. The Night Club Owner observed the outrage and the irrational behavior exemplified by Butch. The ambulance drove him for a mental evaluation, and the doctor prescribed Prozac as medication for Butch. Faith called to the Psychiatric Department at Baptist Hospital in order to see her husband, but the doctor refused to allow her to visit. Rosalind's cousins were members of Mt. Malachi CME Church. The family cliques in the church presented problems for Faith. Isaac confronted Faith at church with information about her adversary.

"My cousin is married to your ex-husband." Isaac said.

"I'm glad that he found someone to love." Faith said.

"My cousin got pregnant by Butch. She had a little girl. You didn't have any children by Butch, but my cousin had the daughter by the rich man." Isaac proudly revealed his cousin's close romantic relationship with Butch.

"I had a miscarriage," Faith admitted while lamenting the loss of her baby by Butch. "Yes, I gave birth prematurely to my fetus. My poor baby didn't live." Faith explained. The enmity toward Eve and Faith in Mt. Malachi CME Church ruffled religious turmoil. Faith and Eve endured the harsh spiritual experiences while worshipping at Mt. Malachi in the heart of the Mound. In the long run, Faith was blessed with a teaching job for Bluff City Schools. The home of the Knights was the new place of her educational abode. Castle High School had a unique architecture. The triple circular architecture of the tan brick Castle had a silver dome roof adorning the building that glittered under the sun. The exquisitely designed building was located on Knightland Avenue. The mascot of the school was a silver metal Knight that stood erect at the entrance of the school. The school was built in 1968. During the 60's, the demographic composition of the Village community consisted of a majority of White upper to lower middle-class homeowners. These were basically blue-color workers. As incomes increased, this group moved to other areas of the city. Low income apartments were erected, and the racial demographics of the community changed. Amid the walls of the Castle lies a mystery about the educational realm. Faith's task was to unlock the key to intellectual development. Her classroom provided a stimulating environment where students acquired learning experiences relating to the real world. Therefore, she designed a variety of innovative cooperative group activities that sparked the interest of her students. Intellectual discrimination caused Faith to encounter many pitfalls during her career in education. Angela Wright's brother, Carlton Wright, worked in the Administrative Office of Bluff City Schools. Willie Lynch's Mentality Doctrine was implemented strongly by Carlton Wright. The Willie Lynch doctrine of differences among Black people instilled envy based upon ignorant verses intelligent. Betsy Kimball warned Faith about a conspiracy against her with members of the Bluff City Schools Administration. Carlton Wright formed an alliance with the principal of Castle High School in order to settle a vendetta on his sister's behalf. The administrators placed many obstacles in Faith's path. Carlton resented the fact that Faith didn't exist in mental darkness void of intellectual light. She was a very good teacher, and her students' Standardize Test scores excelled. Even though Tennessee was an At Will State, Faith was not fired because her evaluations were excellent. Her students worked diligently in preparation for the Standardize Test. The test date was fast approaching. Patsy came into Mrs. Faith Billingston's classroom, and she sat quietly at a desk while working on the assignment. In a twinkling of an eye, a hand emerged from the back of the room.

"Mrs. Billingston, may I go to the restroom?"

"Yes," the teacher said while the student pranced out of the room. In a flash, the intercom system resounded Mrs. Lacey's voice.

"Mrs. Billingston!"

"Yes!" She responded.

"Is Patsy Caldwell in your room?"

"Yes, I let her go to the restroom. Mrs. Lacey, I have a question. Why did you place Patsy in my room a week before the state's test? My students have prepared for the state's test since the beginning of school." Mrs. Billingston inquired about the placement of students.

"Patsy was in a high-level English class. She needed to be in a low-level English class. So, we moved her to your class. It fits her academic level." The Assistant Principal explained the placement procedure at Castle High.

"Ya'll hear what she called us? She called us low-level."
Tiffany said disheartened.

I'm not low-level." Dora said.

"She's saying that we are dumb." Charlotte said. "I ain't
dumb."

"I didn't know this was a low-level class. I don't want to
be in here anymore." Tiffany said desiring to flee from a low-
level academic stigma. Once Mrs. Lacey realized her negative
statement, she summoned Faith Billingston to her office.

"Mrs. Billingston, I want to see you in my office after
school."

"Okay!" Mrs. Billingston said wondering why the
Assistant Principal requested a meeting. Arriving promptly to
Mrs. Lacey's office, the Assistant Principal scolded the teacher

"You should not have asked me about Patsy on the
intercom."

"I wanted to know why she was placed in my room a week
before the Standardized Test. I will be held accountable for her
test score." Mrs. Billingston defended her question.

"We called her mother to schedule an EBE meeting. She
was having trouble with English and math. We considered placing
her in Resource. In order to enroll her in Instructional Resource,
her classes were changed." The Adminstrator explained.

"I don't like the way you insulted my students' academic
ability. You called them low-level on the intercom." Faith
defended her children's academic ability.

"I'm going to write you a letter." The Administrator stated.

"I'm going to write you a letter, too," Mrs. Billingston said while walking out of her office. Faith arrived home, ate dinner, and settled down to write Mrs. Lacey a letter. The next morning, she gave her boss the following letter:

Mr. Lacey, Assistant Principal
1415 Knighland Avenue
Memphis, TN. 38122
Dear Mrs. Lacey:

On March 11, 2000, you pushed the intercom button to room 312 during my Fourth Period. At that time, you asked me if I dismissed Patsy Caldwell to use the restroom. Since Patsy was not originally assigned to my English class, I asked you why she had been placed in my class. You stated over the Intercom that a meeting with the Resource teacher, the Guidance Counselor, as well as yourself decided to move Patsy to a low-level English class. According to you, the class that she was enrolled in was to high level for Patsy. This statement was made in the presence of twenty-five student. The students were outraged at your mentally degrading statement about that class' academic level. You were wrong to deflate my children's academic ability. You were very unprofessional as an educator and an administrator to hurt children. After you realized how you negatively opened your big mouth in front of a whole class, you demanded that I come to your office after school. When I arrived, you wanted to justify your unprofessional remark. Mrs. Lacey, the damage to these children's self-esteem has been done. In light of the fact that our school's name appeared on the Low Scoring List for the Standardize Test, I tried to instill in my student's self-worth. Yet, you tore that down. Children should be encouraged to excel. Mrs. Lacey, you should be woman enough to apologize to that class.

Sincerely,

Mrs. Billingston

On Wednesday morning, Mr. Howard requested that Faith come into his office. When she arrived promptly, he insulted her in front of Carlton Wright.

"Excuse me. Mr. Howard, I am here for the meeting." Mrs. Billingston said.

"I have company. Don't disturb me now. We are looking at a file. You come back later." He said in an arrogant tone. When Mrs. Billingston returned to the principal's office, Ms. Thornton and Mrs. Lacey were sitting in his office adjacent to each other.

"Mrs. Billingston, we are here to discuss the incident between you and Mrs. Lacey. Ms. Thornton is the faculty representative for the BEA. You have the right to have her present, or she may leave." Mr. Howard stated. Mrs. Billingston reminisced about the Laser Disk taken from her room by Ms. Thornton.

"Ms. Thornton gave my Laser Disk to another teacher. She can leave?" As Ms. Thornton walked out wearing her red blouse and black slacks, Faith asked.

"Are you going to be honest?"

"Yes!" She replied.

"You can stay." Mrs. Billingston said. Then, Mr. Howard addressed the letter written to Mrs. Lacey.

"I have no problem with most of the letter. However, I do have a problem with this sentence. You should not have said your big mouth. With all of your education, you could have selected another word. You are reprimanding an administrator." Mr. Howard analyzed the contents of the letter.

"You reprimand her, Mr. Howard. She was wrong. She could've described my students in another way rather than calling them low-level." For the moment, Mr. Howard became angry.

"Now, she is telling me what to do." He said. "Mrs. Lacey, tell Ms. Thornton what is happening." Turning toward he, she said.

"See Patsy…" Faith interrupted Mrs. Lacey before she finished the sentence.

"You need to tell the truth." Faith said assertively. Mr. Howard's voice roared with rage.

"I'm sick of this. This has to stop. I'm sending you to the Board."

"May I go to the Board now?" Faith asked to leave.

"No!" He said. "You get on your post upstairs in your room. You get your butt out of my office, now. Ya'll see; she is belligerent."

"I'm not belligerent. I have not lifted my hand to hit anybody in this office."

"Get out!" He yelled pointing his finger to the door.

"Be patient, Mr. Howard. I've got to get all of my books." Faith said.

"I don't have any patients with you. Go!" He said with a burst of biliousness. Faith grabbed her books hightailing out of there. Mrs. Lacey and Ms. Thornton remained in the principal's office. Upon arriving to her post, she taught a lesson about the Simple Subject. After dealing with the problem at school, Faith dealt with Mrs. Ratchets daughters.

"Hello!" Faith answered.

"Hi Sis! This is Melanie. I called to tell you that our father died."

"Oh! No! I'm sorry to hear that daddy died. I'll tell Man. Have the funeral arrangements been made, yet?" Faith asked.

"We're having a Memorial Service here in Atlanta. Then, we're flying his body to Saginaw, Michigan for the funeral. He will be buried in the same cemetery as Grandma Sally."

"Can you arrange flying privileges for Man and me?"

"I'll check with the Revenue Flying Program for American Airline's employees. They have Plan A, Plan B, and Plan C. The travel perks are usually standby. You only get to travel if there is an open seat on board the aircraft." Melanie explained American Airline's family flying privileges. She continued to discuss their father's Last Will and Testament. "Daddy promised to leave me a thirty-thousand dollars life insurance policy. I might give you and New Baby something since you are his children."

"You don't have to give us a damn thing. Our mother has purchased a nice home for us, and she has given us a good life. Personally, I don't understand why daddy left his insurance policy to the middle child. Why did he overlook Verlie? She is your oldest sister." Faith wondered if her father had a rude awakening about Verlie's paternity. Faith called Verlie the next day to inquire about airline passes to the funeral.

"Did Melanie get an airline pass for Man and me?"

"I am not a message carrier. Don't bother me about an airline ticket for you and your brother." She spurned Faith, and Verlie refused to give her information about the airline.

"This is the second time you've mistreated me. I never will forget the letter written to me years ago. You bragged about the toys daddy brought you for Christmas. You insinuated that we didn't receive toys. Our mother purchased us Christmas gifts every year." Faith said.

"I don't want to be bothered. I personally don't give a damn how you get there." Verlie said.

"You don't have to coup an attitude about the plane ticket." Faith said. Faith's half-sister moved into the step-sister from hell category. Faith hung the phone up immediately, and she called her mother. She told Eve about the problem with transportation to their father's funeral.

"Don't beg them for an airline pass. I'll pay for you and Newton III to attend your father's funeral. I suggest that you all travel on the Greyhound Bus."

"Thank you, momma. I'll call in order to get the price and departure time from Memphis." They purchased the bus ticket, and the siblings traveled to the funeral. While attending the Family Hour, New Baby stood next to his father's casket. Newton Junior's baby sister noticed family hereditary features inherited by New Baby.

"Look at New Baby, Violet. He looks just like Papa Ashwin."

"He does look like our father." Violet agreed. When the Family Hour ended. Verlie confronted Faith about the transportation issue.

"How did you and your brother get to Saginaw?"

"We rode the Greyhound Bus. I asked you to get us an airline pass, but you act nasty." Faith stated.

"That was not my damn problem." Verlie said adamantly.

"Verlie, you know that they were treated badly by you and Melanie. You know how ya'll treated them." The younger sister Marie said. Melanie anticipated inheriting thirty-thousand dollars from her father's life insurance policy. When their father's life insurance policy from American Airlines surfaced, the step-mother was the beneficiary. She did not give Newton's daughters one copper penny. Within the span of time after the funeral, Lawrence and Laura visited Faith to express their condolences.

"Did you get out Sympathy Card?" Laura asked.

"Yes, I appreciate your concern during my time of bereavement."

"We went to Jack Town last weekend. We visited Rosalind while in Jackson. Her daughter is 19 years old now. Time sure flies." Laura said.

"It's tempus fugit." Lawrence used Latin to describe the expeditiousness of time. The conversationalists reported gossip circulating in Jack Town about Butch's daughter.

"I mingled with the guys in Jack Town. They told me about Butch's daughter. The men whispered behind Butch's back about his precious daughter's eroticism. According to my homeboys, Chloe will drop her drawers for anybody. She is always the life of the party." Lawrence said. Years of discretion did not exist in Chloe's teen. The age of indiscretion introduced years of sexual immorality. Lawrence continued to disclose Chloe's sexual powers. "She bragged about possessing great sexual skills. She described fucking hard and fucking long. She fucked while conceiving her first illegitimate child. In the days of yore, Chloe gave birth to her second daughter by Clarence 'Pimp' Wilson. Pimp's drug dealing profession deprived his daughter of child support. Eventually, Chloe dated two guys at the same time. The lovebirds' amorous feelings flew her into Antonio's arms. Antonio's Rap-sheet stretched as long as a football field. He was a career criminal. Deceitfulness caused a misrepresentation of the truth about the fatherhood of her son. In the wake of the birth of Chloe's son, an argument pitted on man against the other man. When she conceived, both men claimed to be the father of the baby boy. Courting Chloe charted Pimp on a collision course. A verbal altercation developed between Antonio and Pimp at the Exxon Gas Station. He was determined to blow out Pimp's brains. Antonio pulled out a revolver killing him with malice. The homicidal maniac slaughtered his romantic competition. The death-dealing gangster mand Pimp's existence devoid of life. He lay lifeless at death's door. When the little boy was born, he resembled Antonio. Rosalind and Chloe moved to Biloxi, Mississippi after that murderous fiasco. Chloe worked at a financial institution in Biloxi, but she could not keep her hands off the money. She was arrested for embezzlement. Butch entered into his second marriage on Valentine Day. He got hitched to Katrina Edwards. She was no virtuous woman. Katrina lived in a married state in Melvin's parents' house without a legal marriage license for years. Two children were born to this union. She entered into a common-law marriage until Melvin died. Butch was the only man to marry a 56-year-old spinster. However, he wasn't stupid enough to marry her without a pre-nuptial agreement. If the marriage ends in divorce, Katrina would leave without any of the Billingston's assets. Laura inserted her input into the conversation.

"Personally, I don't like the way Butch treated his other children. Gloria was the first girl impregnated by Butch. She went to Illinois, and Gloria did not demand child support." Laura stated.

"How old was Gloria at the time of the pregnancy?" Faith asked.

"She was in high school at the time of conception." Laura revealed. "Angela finally had a DNA Test performed in order to prove paternity. Prior to the DNA Test, Angela married a preacher. Reverend Henson raised Butch's daughter as his own child. Honey, Angela started preaching after Reverend Henson's death as a means of releasing her sins. She became holier-than-thou." Laura gave Faith inside info from the grapevine.

"Knowing Angela, she gets up in the Pulpit preaching with a wet ass on Sunday mornings putting on an innocent façade after fucking all night." Lawrence said recollecting Angela's sneaky whorish ways.

"The way Butch disowned her daughter probably caused her to become sanctimonious." Faith surmised. On the next day, Faith confronted the consequences for her actions. Mr. Mallard, a BEA Representative, accompanied her to the meeting at Personnel Services for Bluff City Schools.

"Mrs. Billingston." The receptionist announced.

"Yes, I'm Faith Billingston. This is Mr. Mallard; he is my BEA Representative."

"Mr. Roberts will see you now," the receptionist divulged.

"This is Mr. Marcus Mallard. He represents members of the BEA." She said introducing her anchor of educational strength.

"Mrs. Billingston, I received a fax from Mr. Howard. Your principal alleges that you exemplified unprofessional conduct. You referred to Mrs. Lacey as big mouth."

"Mrs. Billingston documented everything that happened to her at the Castle. In fact, she documented actions by school personnel for decades." Mr. Mallard revealed. At that point, she positioned her gray notebook on top of Mr. Robert's desk. His olive-green eyes flickered with amazement.

"I documented every cruel and harassing remark made to me by Mr. Howard. He harassed me from the first day that I stepped foot in Castle High School. These incidents happened for a long time. However, I don't apologize for calling Mrs. Lacey big mouth. She hurt a classroom full to students by calling them low-level. She degraded their intellectual ability. Mrs. Lacey injured my student's emotional educational stability. Several vocabulary terminologies entered my mind to describe Mrs. Lacey, but big mouth fit the situation perfectly." Faith said candidly.

"Mr. Howard requested that we give you two days suspension without pay." Mr. Roberts revealed.

"Some pilots flew an airplane under the influence of alcohol with hundreds of passengers on board, but they received two days suspension with pay." Faith stated in defense. "Mr. Howard tarnished my clean employment history." She stated.

"With all good consciousness, I can not give you two days without pay," Mr. Roberts said. "I am, however, recommending counseling. I want you to attend Employee Counseling for two days. If you want to continue, you may." He said handing her a business card with the Counselor's name, address, and telephone number. "You may transfer to another school. You may select any school, and I will assign you." Mr. Roberts stated. "When you go back to Castle High, don't call anybody big-mouth."

"Okay," she said smiling. "I won't. Thank you, Mr. Roberts." Faith said gratefully. Mr. Roberts transferred Faith to Centerville High School. The new school assignment placed her in an Optional School; however, Faith did not receive Honor's classes. Since the school's enrollment increased, the Traditional classes had to be leveled to the appropriate size. Faith did not have a permanent classroom. As a floating teacher, she moved from the second floor to the third floor while pushing a cart with books. To make her educational experience easier, Mrs. Lincoln and Mrs. Carter cleaned a small office space for Faith to use as a classroom twice day. The kind, blonde, blue-eyed ladies showed solidarity toward their new co-worker despite racial differences. The Willie Lynch Syndrome placed shackles on people in the job market. African-Americans' forefathers were indoctrinated with these ideologies from birth. Great, great grandmothers implanted the Willie Lynch theory in the psych of their children causing envy against other Blacks. Faith's opposition surfaced when a dark, heavy set co-worker orally attacked her during a Team meeting. In the nick of time, Faith was given four Honor's classes to teach at Centerville.

"Wow! I don't want to meet with her," Wanda Wilbert said. "I hate her. Mr. McDowell gave her all of the Honor's classes. She just got to our school, and I've been teaching here for five years. I can't stay in this meeting."

"I understand," Ophelia Anderson agreed. "It wasn't fair for her to get Honor's classes. We should've been responsible for the mental development of our Honor's students." Ophelia rose to become an Assistant Principal, but she was busted down to the classroom. Faith's academic rivals expressed their resentment. So, Faith talked with the principal about the meeting.

"How in the world will I work with my co-workers? They are highly upset because I have the Honor's classes."

"You must sow the seeds of scholarly success with the Honor's classes. I want you to act professional." The principal advised.

"I will maintain my professionalism." Faith vowed. "Thank you, Mr. McDowell." On a sad occasion, Faith applied for a Family Medical Leave. In the natural course of events, Eve was admitted into the hospital for observation. The Willie Lynch syndrome does not exist in the medical profession. Doctors and Nurse work together to save the life of people from all nationalities. The weekend welcomed a relief for Faith from the conflicts at work. Faith decided to shop until she dropped money at the Mall. While walking through the Mall, she bumped into Vickie.

"Hi Faith! I asked Nancy about you last week. Nancy, Rena and I talked about you on the Three-Way."

"Is discussing me all you bitches got to do?"

"Nancy talked about your marriage to her cousin. According to her, you should've kept your marriage together. You could be working in his family business."

"I didn't marry him in order to work in the family business. That is why I went to college. I wanted my own career."

"He has gotten married again." Vickie said proudly.

"I know about the marriage, and I know about the Pre-nuptial agreement. I'm glad to have my own home. When his marriage ends in divorce or death, she will leave without any property. She will leave like she came with nothing. You always have been messy, Vickie. You kept a mess going when we lived on Clover Street as children."

"I was always jealous of you. You were a cheerleader, and you participated in a lot of activities in high school. I had to baby sit my brothers and sisters." Vickie said. "I'm even mad because your mother is still living and my mother is dead."

"Don't fault me because your mother had seven children by seven different men. All of ya'll got different last names. Your mother taught you well. She took you through whore training." Faith said as she walked away from her enemy. They lynched Faith in the Mound. In the 21st century, African-Americans lynch fellow Blacks at a greater magnitude than the Ku Klux Klan. Inner racism perpetuates envious feeling within the Black community. For spiritual support, Faith attended Winning Christian Church in the suburbs. The shade of differences within the Willie Lynch Syndrome disappeared in the worship services at Winning Christian Church. In the bible belt of the South, this church won souls from all ethnocentric backgrounds. Blacks, Whites, and Hispanics worshipped together in spiritual unity. The diversity of the worship services revealed the true nature of religion. After services, Faith left the sanctuary in a hurry. The pastor hugged a little girl as Faith rushed past him.

"I see you," Reverend Whitmore said while smiling with his light gray eyes looking in Faith's direction. "If I have to run behind you, I will catch you. I am going to greet you." The Caucasian minister overlooked color, and he overlooked racial differences. He stopped Faith, and Reverend Whitmore hugged her. After church, Faith ate dinner at Krystal's. While standing in line, a beggar asked a lady to buy him a cup of coffee.

"Ma'am! Will you buy me a cup of coffee?" The panhandler aske.

"How much does a cup of coffee cost?" She asked.

"Fifty-cents," the cashier answered. Looking perplexed, she reached in her purse, and she gave him some change. The panhandler never uttered: Thank you. Then, the beggar approached Faith.

"Do you have fifty-five cents?" He asked. Faith reached into her pocket, handed him seventy-five cents. In an attempt to teach the nappy headed beggar some manners, she said.

"Thank you!"

"You didn't give me time to say thank you." He said arrogantly.

"The lady gave you money first, but you never told her thank you." He became argumentative. The manager of the restaurant chastised him.

"I can't let you harass my customers." She said.

"Keep your damn cup of coffee." He said while walking out of the restaurant with the change in his hand.

"You can't help some people." The manager explained. "A beggar threw a whole meal in the trash because he wanted the money to buy drugs." She revealed. Faith witnessed Willie Lynch's doctrine of Dependency. According to the Willie Lynch theory, control of the Black man is achieved by making the Black woman independent while making the Black man dependent. As time tipped into Monday afternoon, Faith encountered Jasmine at Fred's Dollar Store.

"Nedra and I started to confront you at your new church. We heard that you left Mt. Malachi CME Church."

"Yes! I left that church. I'd been a member since birth. Who told you about Winning Christian Church?"

"We weren't coming to worship at the church. We decided to park the car at the end of the parking lot."

"You and Nedra are attempting to bully me at my new place of worship. What kind of person would stop someone from worshipping God? It's a damn shame. A person can't worship God in peace." Faith said in spiritual disgust.

"I wanted your assistance with the Wildcat's Den High School's graduation ceremony. We always give a contribution from our class to four graduating seniors bound to college." Jasmine explained.

"Have you ever heard of a telephone? Why park in the church's driveway on a Sunday morning? I paid my fifty dollars dues for our class' Alumni Club. You've never contacted me to participate in our Alma Mater's graduation exercises. Why contact me now? Why would you interrupt me at church?"

"Nedra and I were just having fun talking about you." Jasmine revealed.

"Nedra needs to attend to her business. While she poked fun at me on Nancy's Facebook page, she lost sight of her own home life. She entertained herself for years discussing my defunct marriage to Nancy's cousin Butch. She lost her husband, and she ended in Divorce Court. Most of my classmates are friends with Nancy and Brenda from Hampton High School. I thought Brenda had given up her animosity against me after several years. He wanted Butch, but she lost. All she did was gave up some pussy. Butch married me anyway. You need to take an inventory of your own life. You are fifty-five years old, and you've never been married. You are categorized as an Old Maid. How can you poke fun at me?"

"Faith! You are telling the truth." Jasmine admitted. "Every time classmates come to a meeting, they insult them. They never attend another meeting." Jasmine was a kind-hearted person, but she wanted to be a part of the Wildcat's kitty clique.

"Nancy instigated gossip about my marriage to her cousin for years. Karma is a bitch! Nancy's marriage dissolved after a physical altercation with her step-daughter. The big-time principal of an elementary school experienced domestic violence in her home. The grapevine spread gossip about her ass getting beat while the husband watched. The poor step-daughter reached her limit with Nancy's despicable attitude. She told Nancy the following statement:

"Get your ass out my Momma's house. You dated my daddy while my mom was sick with cancer. You committed adultery. Get out!" She yelled with hostility. "Vickie and Zephyrina have plotted with Nancy for years against me," Faith explained to Jasmine. "It is time for them to stop focusing on my defunct marriage. Jasmine, I've got errands to run. Have a great day."

Chapter 5.

SHACKLES

On the fourth Thursday of November, United States citizens observe a day of giving thanks. The celebration involves a feast with sumptuous food and merrymaking. Eve aroused at 5:00 A.M. to place the turkey in the oven. However, a melancholic mood penetrated the premises. Eve's mind drifted to the week her son and brother died two days apart. A year elapsed, but the pain still lingered in her heart. Newton III and Winston would not be coming to dinner. When Faith awoke about 8:00 A.M., her mother was disgruntled. Eve's soul slid into the depths of depression. She removed the beautifully browned turkey from the oven.

"I don't remember how to make dressing." Eve stated perplexed. "You make the dressing," she instructed Faith. "I've made the corn bread already." Faith never made dressing for Thanksgiving. Her mom prepared the Thanksgiving feast every year. She quickly Googled corn bread dressing recipes, and she printed three recipes. Each recipe possessed a different ingredient, and she did not want to put oysters in her dressing. After mixing the dressing, Faith slid the Bakeware in the oven. Suddenly, the phone rang. Her cousin from Michigan called to wish them a happy Thanksgiving.

"Hey Cuz! How are you?" Marilyn asked.

"I'm fine. I am making the dressing this Thanksgiving. Momma insisted that I make the dressing." Faith said. "She is not slick. Momma's motive involves teaching me how to make dressing," Faith rationalized.

"I cooked a little hen for myself, but I'm going over to my sister Cathy's house. She prepared dinner for the family," Marilyn said.

"I'll call you tomorrow." Faith said. "Bye!" Eve boiled the sweet potatoes in a large pot. When the sweet potatoes softened, her memory lapsed again.

"I can't remember how to make sweet potato casserole." She stated perplexed.

"Momma, you used the following ingredients: a tablespoon of cinnamon, a teaspoon of Vanilla Flavor, a cup of honey, a tablespoon of flour, and an egg. Then, you would mix the ingredients until smooth. After mixing the ingredients, you placed the casserole dish in the oven at 350 degrees."

"You make it." Eve demanded. Faith made the sweet potato casserole, and she placed it in the oven. By that time, Eve became distraught. She began to badger Faith.

"Lynn and Theresa are going to ruin your reputation on Facebook. You built a good reputation for yourself, but they are going to destroy you. That good reputation you built for yourself is going to be torn down, and everybody is going to condemn you. Yeah! Their condemnation of you will hinder you from being what you want in life." Eve antagonized Faith to the utmost degree. Lynn's cousin had exposed her Facebook bullying messages about Faith, and she was aware of the negative comments made against her. Eve prognosticated ill-will on Faith's life. "You're going to have bad luck in life."

"Why are you degrading me? What kind of mother infiltrates her daughter's subconscious mind with negative ideas?" Faith questioned her mom. Faith pleaded with Eve to exemplify some motherly love. "You must be hurting because of the death of our close family members. In reality, we are the only two immediate family members left on earth." Faith attempted to reason with her mother to no avail. "Your words hurt, and they sting deep into my soul, momma." Faith explained.

"You think that I am being hard on you, but the people in the world are going to be even tougher on you. You will have to be strong." Eve stated.

"I realize that a lot of people wish me ill-will. Some even wish me dead, but I expect you to treat me better." Faith reasoned. Eve whined like a two-year-old. The aggressive mannerism changed to a meek childish whine.

"Leave me alone." Eve yelled. "I can't take this anymore. Why are you reminding me about the death of my love ones? I don't want to remember their deaths. It hurts for a mother to experience the death of a child. I've had two sons to die, and my brother. Stop! Shut-up!" A conspicuous cry erupted from her vocal cord. A high-pitched whinny sound enveloped the room with a fit of weeping. Eve sniveled and sniffled while sitting at the kitchen bar. She burst into tears with a loud wailing cry. The childish outcry bewildered Faith. Faith matriculated at Wildcat's Den High School, LeMoyne College, and Trevecca Nazarene University. She received an Educational Specialist Degree from Ole Miss which is the most prestigious university in the nation, but these academic institutions did not train her to deal with the mood swings displayed on this Thanksgiving Day. In April 2013, Eve's doctor's prognosis indicated a small degree of depression and anemia. Eight months later Eve's attitude toward Faith changed dramatically. As her mom's caregiver, Faith worried about the change of attitude toward her success in life. Faith became a teacher, and her brother Newton worked at the Jewish Temple. Newton and Faith fulfilled their mother's dream of writing novels. They wrote novels designed to entertain and inform. Faith's mom never condemned her before now. Faith never lived with condemnation until this phase in life. Eve's grandson arrived for dinner about 3:00 P.M. They enjoyed Thanksgiving dinner, and the food was delicious. On the next day, Faith confronted her mother about the ill-will cast on her by the one individual who should love her.

"Why did you wish ill-will on your own child yesterday? You said that I would have bad luck in life." Faith recollected.

"I didn't say that." Eve said in defense. "I didn't say that," she reiterated with amnesia. Her mental state always denied cruel statements inflicted on her daughter.

"Lynn and Theresa downgraded me on Facebook already. Stewart talked with them on Facebook, and he exposed his Aunt Lynn to me. According to Stewart, she hates me. I have been very good to her son. Since my brother claimed paternity, I accepted him as my nephew. Our family supported him financially and emotionally. Lynn hasn't contributed any financial support for her own son. Stewart showed me Theresa's post on Facebook. Theresa admitted her contempt for our family. I read her comment. According to Theresa, they don't give a damn about our help. She doesn't care about the cars, clothes, and financial support our family gave them. I have given them four cars. She bragged about their family unity. We're Fam," Theresa stated. "Lynn always says that blood is thicker than mud. Our family is mud to her." Faith reminded her mother.

"I don't want to discuss this anymore." Eve ended the conversation, and she went to her room. In the wake of the various mental changes experienced by Eve, Faith accepted a date with Richie. He invited her to the movie.

"Hello Faith! I'm inviting you to the movie. I want to see Thor. The ratings are good, and it is supposed to be an action-packed movie. It starts at 7:00 P.M. I'll pick you up about 6:15 P.M." Richie gave Faith the itinerary for the evening.

"I'm looking forward to seeing Thor. I'll be ready at 6:00." Faith dressed for her date adorned in a flashy, fashionable frock. While putting on her glad rags, Eve entered Faith's bedroom. Sitting on the edge of the bed, Eve began to torment Faith again.

"I don't like you," Eve admitted.

"Why don't you like me? I'm your daughter." Faith reminded Eve. By that time, the doorbell rang. Faith proceeded to the door. Eve came fast tracking behind her with the walking cane.

"I ought to hit him in the back of his head with my cane." Eve said in a pugnacious mode. Faith witnessed a change in her mother's frame of mind. Eve became bellicose, and she gnashed out toward Faith's date in a hostile way. While sitting in the theatre, Eve's belligerent disposition tugged at Faith's heart. Her mother's attitude changed to an argumentative, aggressive human being that Faith did not recognize. Upon arriving home from the movie theatre, panic penetrated Faith's mind. She mused about Eve's loss of memory on Thanksgiving Day. Faith's mind recollected the contempt expressed by her mom. She became apprehensive about sleeping in a house with someone's hatred. A gun in the hands of an enemy scared the shit out of Faith. She locked the door to her bedroom, and she tried to enter the Land of Nod. However, her body was deprived of rest. The unnerving thought of a gun in an elderly person's hand made Faith's flesh creep. An eerie feeling frightened her. There was no rest for the weary. In the wake of being the object of hatred, Faith's dismay left a panic-stricken mental impression. She walked slowly towards her mother's room with a Nine Millimeter in hand. Eve was startled. The sight of a gun impressed Eve with fear. The frightening vision of a Nine Millimeter sparked a horrifying nightmare in her mind. Faith laid the gun on her mother's bed. She demanded vehemently that Eve give the antique 22 caliber pistol to her, but she could not reason with Eve.

"Give me your gun," Faith demanded.

"I don't have my gun." Eve said in denial.

"Where is your gun?" Faith questioned.

"Stanley has my gun." She admitted. The matriarch of the family objected to giving the pistol to her daughter. Faith's intentions were honorable, but Eve was terrified. In a split second, the little old lady sprang into action. Eve moved with extreme quickness, grabbed the gun, and held the weapon in the air toward the ceiling. Instantaneously, Faith jumped from her seat on the bed. She grasped her mother's hand forcefully until she released the weapon. Faith snatched her mother's hand, and she walked swiftly pulling her mother from the bedroom. In the meantime, the security system started ringing. Faith entered the security numbers in order to dislodge the alert message. She ushered her mother to the garage, and they drove away. Faith directed the course of the automobile toward her mother's house. Eve purchased and paid the 30-year mortgage on a modest red brick home in the Grove subdivision. Faith pulled into the driveway, and she made the following request:

"Momma! I want you to stay at your house for a minute. I'm going back home to search for your gun."

"I'm not going in there," Eve said adamantly. "Stanley has my gun." She admitted. On the spur of the moment, Faith went into the house to jog Stanley's memory. Stan was sleeping late as usual.

"Stan! Do you have momma's gun?"

"Gun!" He asked flabbergasted. The gun question threw Stanley for a loop. He set up erect in the bed dumfounded.

"No! I don't have momma's gun."

"Okay! Momma lied." Faith said as she exited the residence. In a flash, Faith zipped down Lamar Avenue to the Fire Station. A big yellow sign with large black letters stated Safe Place.

"Momma, the Fire Station is a Safe Place. I want you to stay here until I find your gun. Stan said that he doesn't have your gun. Since he is a felon, Stan can't have a weapon."

"I'm not going in there. Take me to the Police Station."

"Momma, I'm not driving to the Police Station."

"I want the police." Eve demanded.

"Call the police on your cell phone, momma. If you want to call the police on me, dial 911." Eve dialed the three digits, and three white police cars with large royal blue letters spelling the words Memphis Police on each side appeared in the Fire Station's parking lot. Faith walked toward the officers, placed her hands behind her back, and positioned herself to be arrested. In the meantime, Eve arouse from the car to talk with the officers. The cops detained Faith in the back of the police car. A seat of dignity was non-existent in this vehicle. The hard silver-metal seat-imposed pain on Faith's ass. Since Faith lost several hours of sleep worrying about her mom's mood swings, her body was deprived of sleep. She caught a few Z's. Faith exchanged a soft cushion bed for hard metal ware. The lawmen placed her under arrest, and she was taken into custody. The fuzz drove her to 201 Poplar. The officers drove into the Sally Port which is a large garage like structure. They guided Faith into the elevator to a second-floor office area. They parked her on a long silver metal seat, and they handcuffed her right leg to the metal bench. The two uniform officers sat at a desk. After 30 minutes, Faith spoke.

"I hate to disturb you," she said to the lawmen while squirming in her seat. "I have to urinate." She needed to piss at that very moment.

"I can't take you to the ladies' room. A female officer must take a lady to the restroom," the cop informed her. Faith wiggled and twisted in the seat from embarrassment.

"Can that lady take me to the restroom?" She asked pointing to an office worker. "I will not run away. I promise," Faith assured the officers of her integrity.

"Excuse me, young lady! Will you take our prisoner to the ladies' room?" The officer asked.

"Yes!" The office worker agreed. The policeman unlocked the handcuffs from Faith's ankles. Faith returned from the lavatory, and she played the waiting game.

"When will Transport come to take her to Jail East? We can be on patrol." The officer requested information.

"They should have been here. My patience is wearing thin." His partner said while texting on his cell phone. At long last, a young African-American officer about 40 years old and a Caucasian officer about 50 years old with gray hair came to transport Faith to Jail East. The black officer unlocked the handcuffs from her ankle, and he placed handcuffs around her wrist behind Faith's back.

"We're here to pick up the prisoner."

"She's here," he said pointing at the suspect.

"We are releasing her in your custody." The Shelby County Sheriffs boarded the elevator with Faith, and they departed the Criminal Justice Center. The elderly officer held Faith's arm while strolling speedily from the building. Her pace was pretty damn quick, and the old White gentleman could barely move expeditiously.

"Don't let her leave you, Man!" The young officer directed his comrade. "Keep up with her. Walk fast with her."

"I've got his, Man! I'm in control." The Sheriff Deputy's prance accelerated hastily. During the lapse of time driving to Jail East, the young Sheriff seized a chance to type the report of Eve's version about the gun episode.

"Are you typing momma's opinion of what happened?" Faith asked while peeping over his shoulder.

"Yes! Your mother admitted that both of you had a gun."

"I'm glad that she told the truth." Faith said. The white Sheriff Department's van adorned with olive green and bright yellow letters pulled into the Sally Port near the Penal Farm. The officers frisked Faith. They searched her quickly for contraband.

"Mrs. Billingston! Why are you in jail?" The Sheriff Deputy asked.

"My mother and I had a disagreement, and guns were involved. I don't understand why she forgets simple things. She forgot how to make dressing on Thanksgiving Day."

"I know that shocked you. Your mother has made dressing all your life." The officer's intuition was keen.

"You are right. Momma has cooked dressing every Thanksgiving. She is a good mother, but I'm afraid of her memory lost. She scolded me about my ability to achieve. According to her, I'll never be what I want to be in life. Momma never degraded her children." Faith said.

"Mrs. Billingston, you have already accomplished a lot in life. You've had a great career." The Sheriff's Deputy praised Faith.

"Momma said that she didn't like me." Faith lamented.

"Don't believe that statement. Your mother loves you." The Sheriff Deputy assured her. "Who is your pastor?"

"Reverend Patterson is my minister." Faith answered.

"I am a minister." The female sheriff informed her.

"Pray for me." Faith asked for a devout petition to God on her behalf. Out of the blue, a young female deputy came into the Holding Cell.

"Mrs. Billingston, your mother probably has early signs of Dementia. My aunt's mental state showed signs of Dementia. Her daughter refused to keep my aunt. So, we let my aunt move with my mom and me. My aunt became violent, and we had to put her in a Nursing Home." Memphis police officers proved to be fine human beings. The law enforcement officers treated Faith with respect; they were humane. A pregnant female rested in the Holding Tank with Faith. The mother appeared to be eight months pregnant.

"Oh!" The mother wailed a war cry against pain. "My back hurts so bad." She whimpered. "I need to lie down on this bench." Everybody moved allowing the mother to recline on the hard-concrete bench. The prisoners were detained in the Holding Tank for two hours. Upon release from the Tank, the captives sat in a large waiting room. The arrested development procedures required prisoners to experience jail protocol. The Book was thrown at each convict. The Shelby County Correctional Facility recorded charges against each captive. When officers Book people in jail, an impression of the lines and whorls on the inner surface of each finger is used for the identification of each person. The officers took the fingerprints of the prisoners, and they processed paper work in order to place every possible pertinent charge against an accused person. A mug shot captured a photograph of the face of the suspects. Pictures were taken for police records. The pictures were placed on plastic wrist bands worn by criminals. Faith's picture was not a Glamour Shot. Her deep-set eyes disclosed dark circles from the lack of sleep. She realized the necessity of using concealer and make-up when your ass goes to jail. Some of the ladies smiled on their mug shots, but Faith didn't see a damn thing to smile about being photographed for the Just Busted Magazine. The officers seized unattached hair.

"If your weave comes off when I pull, the hair is mine." The Sheriff warned. Faith wore her hair in a ponytail, but the officer demanded that the band be removed from the ponytail. The young ladies socialized while waiting to undergo the Booking Process. A young lady wearing a fire red weave ignited a conversation with Faith.

"What are you doing here? You look like a nice person. You should be home watching T.V."

"I'm charged with Domestic Violence assault." Faith answered.

"Who did you assault?" Faith refused to disclose the victim. However, little Red Riding Weave speculated about the identity of the victim. "She assaulted her man. She kicked his ass." She said laughing. "When I get out of jail, I'm going to Arizona. You can get a prescription for marijuana from the doctor for anything. If you tell the doctor that your toe hurts, he will prescribe marijuana to cure your hurting toe."

"I heard that Arizona is a beautiful place." A young prisoner said describing the aesthetics of Arizona. The span of time under legal restraint allowed inmates to have a physical medical exam. Inmates are given a pregnancy test, a blood pressure level test, an oxygen level test, and checked for a weak heart caused by heart disease.

"Mrs. Billingston, report to Medical." The nurse summoned Faith to the office.

"You are not pregnant." She said.

"Ha! Ha! Ha!" Faith laughed. "I knew that the pregnancy test would be negative." At her age, it was impossible for Faith to conceive.

"Your heart rate is fine, and your oxygen level is extremely high." The nurse diagnosed.

"What does the oxygen level mean?" Faith asked.

"The level sends oxygen to the brain. An individual's oxygen level must be between 92 and 100 in order to be normal." The nurse explained.

"I'm glad that my vital signs are okay." Faith said. At that point, the nurse called the next inmate for a physical. Faith sat quietly listening to the inmates' conversations. A sheriff's deputy called Fait to a secluded area.

"You have to dress-out. You have to wear jail attire, but I need to check you first. You must undress." She instructed Faith. "Bend over, and I want you to touch your toes." Faith turned her buttocks upward. "Now, I want you to cough."

"Hawk! Hack!" In a sudden noisy manner, Faith's throat expelled air from her lungs.

"Why do I have to turn my rump upward and cough?" She asked the deputy.

"If an inmate placed drugs in their buttocks, the contraband will come out when the prisoner coughs," she answered. "You may leave, Mrs. Billingston. Go to the uniform room to get your outfit." Faith walked to the Uniform Room, and she received a bright orange shirt, black pants, and orange plastic flip-flops. A cell number and a bunk bed assignment were given to her. Faith dwelled in a cell like a bird that could not fly. She resembled a jailbird caged in a coop with the cell block number 14 affixed on the door. Faith's cell mate welcomed her to their place of abode. Her Celly, a name used for a cell mate, was a young White girl with light brown hair and pretty brown eyes.

"Hi! I'm Erica. Why are you in here?" She asked.

"Domestic Violence assault is my charge." Faith answered. "Why are you here?" Faith returned the question.

"Assault!" She answered. "I got my ass in this shit because of my boyfriend. I tried to fuck him and his new girlfriend up. I should've left their ass alone. I wouldn't be here. He got me on Meth. He deals methamphetamine, and he is a tattoo artist. Look at by tattoos." She raised her arms, and she raised the back of her orange jail house blouse. A beautiful colorful tattoo covered her back. Celly explained the jail protocol to Faith. "You must make your bed every morning, and you can't have a wrinkle in your blanket. Your bed has to be made properly. If not, the guard will throw your mattress on the floor. You will pick the mattress up, and you will remake your bed." Erica further schooled Faith. "You can't spit in the Face Bowl after brushing your teeth, either. You have to spit in the toilet. Hang you bath towel and face cloth here," she said pointing at some metal hooks attached to the wall. Exhaustion crept over Faith's conscious state of mind. A dark gray colored steel bunk bed provided a place of rest for the cellmates. Faith was assigned the bottom bunk to recline from dusk to dawn.

"Where is my pillow?" Faith asked Celly. "I see the pillow case, but there is no pillow." Faith maintained.

"We don't have a pillow. You have to make a pillow."

"How can I make a pillow?"

"Take your top sheet, and fold it into the pillow case," Erica explained. During the hours of darkness, Faith could not fall asleep. Her slumber tie was agitated by the light. The dim-light stayed on all night. Faith attempted to cover her eyes with the old gray blanket. The light aggravated her source of serenity in the dark hours. Erica, on the other hand, slept sound. Faith tossed and turned on the tissue thin mattress. Shower time presents cleanliness at 7:00 o'clock at night or 7:00 o'clock in the morning. Faith elected to shower in the morning. After showering, she instinctively stepped out nude to dry-off with a white towel.

"You can't step outside of the shower to dry your body, Mrs. Billingston." The guard scorned her for exposing her body.

"If you're Horney ladies, you know what needs to be done to have an organism in the shower." The guard further advised the inmates. Faith gained knowledge about the water trick from a sexual book published years ago. Hence, she was aware of sexual water sensations. "You can't have consensual sex in here, either." The guard warned against lesbian sexual acts. On the real tip, Faith's sexual preference required the penetration of a dick. She enjoyed the real deal not a strap-on-penis. However, Faith didn't discriminate against gays and lesbians. She respected all human beings. The first meal of the day provided oatmeal, coffee, and toast. Faith consumed breakfast, but the bologna sandwich for lunch was distasteful. She never liked bologna, and she refused to devour the sandwich. The bag of potato chips and juice were consumed for nourishment. A prisoner sitting across the table from Faith noticed her untouched sandwich.

"You don't want your sandwich?" She observed.

"No! I don't like bologna."

"Give me your sandwich," she begged.

"Okay!" Faith agreed while allowing her to take the sandwich from the tray. "What is your name?"

"I'm Coco," she said introducing herself. Coco, a heavy-set black woman, gobbled up all Faith's unwanted food. Since Faith was on a diet, she refused to eat pork and beef. The penitentiary did not serve a blue-plate special. The inmates were not given an expensive restaurant meal. They didn't even receive salt and pepper to season the food. Faith decided to eat alacarte.

She ate separate items on the menu. For the time being, Coco sat in close proximity to Faith at every meal. When Faith and Erica returned to their cell, Celly gave Faith some advice.

"Don't give her all your food. You need to eat your own food. You are going to be hungry."

"I don't have an appetite. I'm just not hungry. I'll give Coco my food. If I don't eat the food, the meal will be thrown away." From that time forth, Coco ate all Faith's unwanted food. Inmates lingered in the lounging area during certain times of the day. The guards allowed them to socialize about two hours a day. During the fellowship hour, the prisoners socialized developing a circle of acquaintances. On the second day of imprisonment, Faith fraternized with the inmates.

"Hi! I'm Donna. What's your name?"

"I'm Faith."

"Why are you in jail?"

"I was arrested for Domestic Violence assault." Faith revealed.

"Who did you assault?" Donna drilled Faith for an answer.

"I'm here for assaulting my mother." Faith disclosed.

"You assaulted your mother!" Donna asked surprised.

"Yes! I asked my mother for her gun, but she refused to give me the weapon. My mom showed signs of memory lost during Thanksgiving Holidays. I'm afraid to live in the house with a gun in her possession. She didn't remember how to make dressing for Thanksgiving."

"My mother is dead." Donna said. "I took care of her until she died."

"I love my mother," Faith admitted. "I just don't know how to deal with her mood swings."

"You'll need to be patient with her." Donna advised.

"Why are you in jail?" Faith countercharged.

I'm here for Domestic Violence assault, too." Donna acknowledged.

"Who did you assault?"

"I pulled a gun on my boyfriend's best friend. That White boy talked to me stupid in my own house. I went off completely. Nobody can talk to me disrespectful in my house." Donna sounded out an answer. "What is your bond?" Donna bombarded Faith with questions.

"I don't know. I don't have a bond." Faith admitted.

"The judge will set a bond for you. Do you have anybody to pay your bail?"

"No! I don't have anybody to pay my bail. I don't have any family except my mom. My brothers are dead, and my uncle is dead."

"You've got God. God put you here for a reason. You need to form a relationship with the Lord." Donna proclaimed.

"I'm Ms. Hendricks. Let me give you something. You need to read this information. This message will help you survive your ordeal. Ms. Hendricks flipped the pages in the Bible to a passage, and she said "read James, Chapter verses through." Ms. Hendricks imparted spiritual guidance to Faith. Faith read the following passage: Dear brothers, is your life full of difficulties and temptations? Then be happy, for when the way is tough, your patience has a chance to grow. So, let it grow, and don't try to squirm out of your problems. For when your patience is finally in full bloom, then you will be ready for anything, strong in character, full and complete. (James 1: 1-4). The scripture from the Living Bible gave Faith spiritual upliftment. The prisoners were more spiritually in tune with God than the church whores attending Mt. Malachi CME Church every Sunday. A young lady with a quiet demeanor sat next to Faith at the circular table.

"Why are you in jail?" Faith asked.

"I'm charged with murder," she said divulging the possibility of a manslaughter conviction. After the realization of a murder charge silence surrounded the table with speechlessness. The gregarious union among the inmates ended when the Sheriff opened the cell chamber doors. When the cell block shut down, Faith conversed with her cellmate. Erica uncovered inside information about another prisoner. She pointed to a cell in full view of their compartment.

"Do you see the lady with blonde hair in the cell across from us?"

"Yes, I see her. Who is she?"

"She got busted for marijuana while driving through Millington. They gave her twenty days for a bag of marijuana."

"I wouldn't want to get busted for drugs in Millington." Faith said. "Isn't a bag of marijuana a misdemeanor?"

"I don't know the charge for possession of a bag of Weed." Erica confessed. Officer Kelsey released Faith to a special department. The turnkey unlocked the cell door.

"Mrs. Billingston, they want you in room 211." Officer Kelsey said.

"Where is room 211?" Faith asked.

"Go through the double doors, and turn left. You will report to that office." Faith pondered the nature of her visit while walking slowly down the hall. A row of chairs lined the wall. One young lady about five feet tall sat in the first seat. Faith sat next to her.

"Hi! Why are you in jail?" Faith asked.

"I got busted for sucking a dick in public," she admitted. "Why are you here?"

"I got arrested for Domestic Violence." Faith informed her. "Why were we called to this room?" Faith questioned.

"We have to be tested. They will give us a Syphilis test and an AID's test. If you test positive for one of those sexually transmitted diseases, you will stay locked up for 11 months and 29 days," she said. The nurse called the dick sucker into her office, drew her blood, and released her to the cell block. Faith entered the Health Department, and her blood was drawn to be tested.

"Call the Health Department in order to get your results. You must give them your Booking Number."

"Okay!" Faith said taking the light blue card. The ravages of time moved at a snail's pace on the third day of Faith's incarceration. The daily routine of shower time, meal time, and communal time paved the way for the house of detention to charge taxpayers for inmates' lockup time. The social circle in the penitentiary provided freedom from distress for Faith. She found a genuine camaraderie in prison rather than the fake alliances with the Black bourgeoisie bitches in the educational arena. Faith taught school in the Bluff City for 30 years, but she never developed a close relationship with teachers. Faith retained a professional relationship with co-workers and students. The criminal social circle welcomed her with opened arms.

"Where do you work?" Latasha asked.

"I'm a retired teacher." Faith revealed.

"Where did you teach?"

"I taught at several schools." The inmates were congenial, and Faith enjoyed the friendly atmosphere.

"If you want your hair braided, you need to move to the front table," Officer Kelsey said. A special area accommodated the female inmates' desire for beauty preparation. The beauty booth was a circular table in the eating section of the cell block. The ladies braided hair in the cosmetology region. Faith touched her dry, wavy hair, and she decided to get braids.

"Will you braid my hair?" She asked Latasha. "I like your braids," she said admiring the young twenty-year old's pretty hairdo.

"Yes! How do you want your hair braided?"

"I like your braids. I want my hair styled similar to your braids." The young jailhouse beautician braided Faith's hair with an upsweep of braids along with a pompadour on top of her head. After the beautician finished Faith's braids, they devoted time to playing cards.

"Let's play Spades." Latasha suggested.

"I'll be your partner." Faith requested. "We need two partners. Who will be our opponents?"

"Keisha and Janice can be partners," Latasha said. The four players formed a partnership. The partners sat opposite each other.

"Latasha, you deal." Keisha demanded. The cards were shuffled, and Latasha dealt the cards in a clockwise order beginning with Keisha on the dealer's left. Keisha called upon her partner to bid on the number of trick books.

"How many books do you see? Please don't tell me nil books. I know that you see more than zero books."

"I see three trick books," her partner bided.

"We're going board," Keisha said.

"I see five books," Faith observed.

"We're going for seven trick books," Latasha stated. Faith began to hoodwink her opponents.

"Jump high or stay at home," Faith made a wager.

"Play a trick and get a treat," her partner challenged. Once the partners' played their cards throughout the game, Faith and Latasha won the game.

"Rise and fly." Faith spoke loudly. At that moment, Officer Kelsey endured the boisterous card players long enough.

"You have been too loud. Everybody go back to your cell. I might let y'all out thirty minutes later." The deputy said. At the point of time, Officer Kelsey released the inmates from their cells thirty minutes later. Faith walked toward the deputy showing the universal hush symbol with her index finger pointed against her lips.

"I'll be quiet," Faith told Officer Kelsey.

"Mrs. Billingston, you are so country. You were really loud." Officer Kelsey said smiling.

"I'll be citified." Faith assured the guard. The shade of night called to mind thoughts of Erica's children.

"I miss my children." Erica called to mind. "Christmas will be here in a couple of weeks, and I need to be with my children."

"How many children do you have?" Faith asked.

"I've got two children," Erica disclosed.

"How old are your children?"

"They are two and five years old. I need to get them some Christmas toys. My momma will get them some Christmas toy, but I need to do my part." Erica insinuated. After a brief conversation, the inmates retired in the condition of repose called sleep. Faith and Celly fell into a deep sleep. The peep of morning presented Faith with a trip from the prison to the Criminal Justice Center at 201 Poplar Avenue. Inmates' names were called, and the turnkey unlocked ten cell doors. On account of the frigid December temperature, the convicts dressed in heavy orange jackets. Officer Henry put the ladies in restraints. Officer Henry put ladies in restraints.

"Come on, baby!" Officer Henry's terms of endearment made Faith feel at ease. She was kind even though Faith was older than the deputy. All at once, Faith raised her jail house pants legs up to be shackled.

"No!" Donna yelled. "Don't lift your pants legs up. The shackles will hurt because the metal will rub against your skin. You will be in pain. Pull your pants legs down low, and let the guard put the handcuffs around your pants."

"Thanks, Donna!" Faith said grateful to her friend for the advice. "I hate shackles." Faith thought. Silver bracelets handcuffed both wrist with a chain extending down to Faith's ankles connecting the silver bracelets to her feet. "I ain't going to be able to run... I ain't going to be able to walk with a stroll." Faith analyzed the situation in her mind. Faith was shackled down to the ground. Shackles hindered the movement of people since slavery times. Moving into the Penal System, shackles bound the prisoners by restricting movement while incarcerated. The ladies hobbled to the Sally Port, and they boarded the Sheriff

Department's bus. Donna sat next to Faith, and a conversation ensued about being a caretaker of elderly parents.

"I kept my mother until she died," Donna said. "I bathed her, and I fed her like a baby. I even cleaned her after bowel movements. You will need to be patient with your mother. When she has a mood change, talk to her with enduring words. Call her sweetie or call her darling. She will respond with a positive disposition." Prior to entering the courtroom, the shackles were removed. The convicts completed an application unveiling their source of income. They marked a section for a Disability Check or a Social Security Check. Then, the captives paraded one by one into the Court of Domestic Relations. At that time, the judge reviewed their financial affairs. A vast majority of the inmates were granted a Public Defender. However, the judge probed deeper into the source of Faith' finances. The bailiff ordered her to approach the bench. The judge questioned Faith about her money.

"Mrs. Billingston, do you get a Social Security check?"

"Yes, sir."

"I know that you receive more than $600.00 dollars a month. How much do you get a month?"

"I get over $3,000.00 dollars a month."

"You can afford to pay for a lawyer," the judge said scrutinizing Faith's money matters. Upon arriving back to Jail East, the inmates attended church services. The make-shift sanctuary was a room with thirty chairs. Reverend Howard placed his CD player on the table.

"I'm going to play a religious song to set a spiritual atmosphere. This song will ignite a religious frame of mind within your soul." The prisoners listened to a Gospel song entitled 'God Will Make a Way' by Don Moen. The minister's sermon focused on denouncing the flesh, and the message focused on uplifting one's spiritual walk. The preacher prognosticated about the future plans of an inmate.

"A young lady sitting in this room plan on leaving town after being released from jail. You need to stay in Memphis. Don't run from your problems. You will encounter the same problem in New York. You need to get saved. Don't worry! Your jail record will be clean." The preacher's prognosis revealed Faith's innermost motives. Her plans were to escape from Memphis. The time devoted to dinner witnessed a verbal altercation. Keisha initiated a belligerent brawl. A false accusation provoked a sharp retort from her.

"Tell the truth, bitch!" Keisha stated improperly using the King's English. "I'll kick your ass," she threatened.

"Go for it, whore!" Morgan invited her to an ass kicking show. "Don't write a check with your mouth that your ass can't cash," Morgan said.

"We can go to Knuckle City, bitch," Keisha said. "You need to stop lying," she warned. "I hate you, motherfucker." Keisha expressed her hatred for her nemesis.

"Damn you, Keisha! I'm not lying." Morgan defended herself against the accusation. In the thick of the conflict, the young ladies almost engaged in a tussle. They were about to scrap when Faith interrupted before they exchanged blows.

"Keisha move! You're going to get in trouble. I'll sit at your table." Faith said while picking up her food tray.

"Okay! I'll move before I fuck this whore up," Keisha said. When the seating arrangement changed, Officer Kelsey objected.

"Don't change seats. Once you sit at a particular table, you must occupy that seat." Officer Kelsey cautioned. The potential fisticuffs episode ceased. The prison inmates were sent to their cells after dinner. As soon as the inmates returned to their cells, Keisha brought Faith a paper towel full of Golden Flakes Jalapeno Cheddar Cheese Puffs and some Ginger Snap cookies. Faith appreciated the snacks because she didn't have any commissary. The house of correction used a computerized system to order snack and supplies, but Faith didn't have any money on the Books. She shared the snacks with Erica, and they enjoyed eating the treats. When the long hand on the clock struck eight, the sheriff called Faith with good news. Somebody posted bail for her through Bluff City Bail Bond Company. All the inmates heard the announcement about her release. Donna signaled for Faith to get her Booking number. Officer Kelsey forbid them from exchanging numbers.

"No! Y'all can't interact. Go on! You can get her number," she said giving her approval.

"Thank you!" Faith said receiving Donna's booking number. Everybody walked to their cell doors cheering and waving bye to Faith.

"Don't come back," an inmate yelled. Faith retrieved her clothes, and she waited for a ride home. Eve posted bail for her daughter, and she sent Stan to pick Faith up from Jail East.

"Momma couldn't rest. She worried everyday about you being incarcerated," Stan said.

"I haven't socialized with young ladies in years. I enjoyed myself. The girls were friendly. They treated me nice." Faith said. Suddenly, Marvin Sapp's song entitled "The Best in Me" played on the radio. This song described explicitly the life experiences endured by Faith. Faith was footloose and fancy free without shackles keeping her in captivity. Faith's social status diminished in the eyes of her classmates. During the monthly class meeting, Zephyrina lunged at Faith's legal matters with a hostile intent. She threw Shade casting a dark shadow around Faith's life behind bars. The female version of Zephyr went into a jealous rage at the Wildcat's Den's alumni meeting. As the Greek legend goes, Zephyr threw a discus killing Hyacinthus. Zephyrina killed the reputation of Faith in the class meeting. Patsy called the meeting to Order. Cheryl read the Minutes from the last meeting. The members discussed the Scholarship contributions given to the Wildcat's Cubs graduating during the current school year. At that point, Zephyrina pounced upon Faith's legal problems.

Orange Mound Community Center donates tooth paste to the prisoners in jail every year. I just thought you needed to know. I just threw that information out there." In an underhanded ploy, Zephyrina leaked Faith's jail incident. However, the classmates were not weak minded enough to entertain Zephyrina's negative thoughts. The young ladies treated Faith with love and respect.

Chapter 6.

THE HEARING ROOM

Entering into 201 Poplar, everyone lined in two rows in order to be scanned for contra-band. Each person walked through the Rapiscan System Meter 250 in search of weapons. A Faith's black bag rolled down the conveyor belt, a fork was discovered by the camera a it zooms photos of the contents in her bag. She packed some strawberries and pineapple to eat for breakfast. The fork was confiscated. All contra-band was confiscated. Faith boarded the elevator to the Second Floor. In the meantime, a female bailiff wearing a tan Shelby County Government emblem on the sleeve and an olive-green pair of pants stood in front of the Hearing Room door. The hall was crowded, and all of the silver metal seats were occupied except one chair. Faith quickly grabbed that seat. The bailiff's dingy-blonde bob-cut hair glimmered while she called the roll for people seeking Protection Orders.

"There are 80 names on this docket. You need to be patient while I call the roll," she commanded. "You must answer present for me to check your name off the list," the bailiff instructed. As Faith's eyes roamed around the room, she viewed a young lady with a maroon sweat shirt with the restaurant Wendy's name printed in bold white letters. She desired a Chicken Portabella sandwich, but the big sign banned food. The sign read as follows: No Smoke, No Food, or Drinks on this floor.

Faith's attorney, Matthew Robinson, showed up to give her legal encouragement. He was immaculately dressed with a three-piece gray-pin stripe suit, white shirt, and matching gray neck-tie. He was a distinctive young with a light-brown beard and pretty green eyes.

"Hello Faith," Attorney Robinson said greeting her. "You are facing 3 to 15 years in prison if convicted of Aggravated Assault with a deadly weapon. I want you to know that this is the easy part. I will be in court this morning, but call me on my cell when you leave." He said. After Faith's attorney left the Hearing Room, a young lady occupied the seat next to her. The young lady had a problem with people discussing her case on Facebook. "Yes, he was served." She informed the noisy person on the other end of the phone. "The Protective Order should keep him away from me. I don't want to see him anymore. I am not supposed to talk with him, nor am I supposed to talk with his friends. His friend messaged me through Facebook seeking information from me about the incident. She claimed to have my best interest at heart. I don't trust her. She said that she would keep my information confidential. The only person that I have confidence in is myself," she said pledging allegiance to herself. At that moment, Faith's mother entered the Hearing Room being pushed in her wheelchair by her grandson. He attended to Grandma Eve's every need. Suddenly, a well-known attorney entered the court room. Faith remembered his face from several high-profile cases.

"Bout time you showed-up," the bailiff said to Attorney Barton.

"I love you, too." Attorney Barton said walking into the court room. Conversations permeated the room. A young lady from Arkansas had a case in Memphis. Evidently, she had an altercation with a resident in the Bluff City.

"You know family members love putting charges on you," she said to her companion. Her companion with a short gray Afro hair style nodded in agreement.

"That's why I stay by myself," she replied while holding her silver walking cane. Meanwhile, a young black man wearing an old-fashion Dallas Cowboy blue and white jogging suit entered the room. He wore his white baseball cap turned backward. This energetic spirit entered the premises while talking on his cell phone.

"Hey momma! They got me up here on some bull-shit. I'll call you back when I leave." Cowboy said terminating the phone call. The bailiff walked over to a young heavy-set light-skinned lady holding a two-year-old little girl. She handed the little girl the roll, and the child grabbed the roll from her hand. Then, the little girl laughed, and she handed the roll back to the bailiff. Afterward, a lawyer approached a young white girl with long light-auburn hair. He informed her about the case.

"Lawyers are here for both sides. We will be prepared. I wanted you to know what to expect."

After her attorney left, she took out her yellow cell phone. She called someone in order to keep them abreast of events transpiring about the case. Since this was the season to be jolly, a lady with a navy-blue Christmas sweater embellish with Christmas trees and Santa Clause gave out brochures. The brochure listed some Safety Net Services and Community Resources. In the meantime, Cowboy roamed the range with vim and vitality. This human dynamo wasn't shy about approaching the bailiff.

"Call me next." He demanded. "I'm just trying to get in and out." He told the bailiff. Another animated character sat next to the Hearing Room door encouraging Cowboy on to liven-up the area. Wearing a black tee shirt with large gold letters with the number nine printed in front, the young man looked like he was ready for combat with his pants tucked in his boots.

"Man! Remember what Kevin Hart says. This is a serious situation, dude." He informed Cowboy. The dynamic duos enliven the whole Hearing Room area. Number Nine continued to converse with Cowboy. "I'm ready like Freddie. I'm ready to get this Protective Order. I'm ready to vamp." Number Nine said.

"I ain't put nothing on nobody." Cowboy said declaring his innocence. "They put it on men. I'm going to get the judge to squash this shit." Cowboy said full of pep. While sitting next to a young man wearing a Fed Ex jump suit, Faith beamed into his conversation. A noisy friend walked over to him in order to delve into his business.

"What's up my Nigger?" He greeted his friend with a racial term of endearment. African-Americans refer to each other as Nigger on a daily basis with a badge of pride and honor. However, the 'N' word should never be leaked from the lips of a human being from another race. The 'N' word is taboo. Black folks use racist names for White folks without any public consequences. Black folks call White folks the following racist names within their own social groups: Red-necks, Honkies, and Crackers. The nosey Joker probed deeper into his friend's business.

"What about your gun charge?" He inquired.

"I'd rather not bring that up." He said refusing to discuss the case.

"How's your sister?" Mr. Nosey asked.

"She fine. She tried to steal from me, man." Mr. Fed Ex informed him about his sister taking something from him.

"You need to get on her good side. Man, look like you going to be here for a minute. I'll talk with you later." He said as he left the Hearing Room. At that point, the bailiff called for John McCray.

"John McCray," the bailiff summoned. However, John did not answer. "If John McCray is not present, I'm going to ask for a warrant for his arrest." The bailiff prepared to issue a warrant for John's arrest. Later, John McCray appeared in the Hearing Room. He quickly informed the bailiff of his presence.

"What you said!" Number Nine yelled using the latest slang. At that point, the bailiff called for the young lady from Arkansas.

"Cathy Sanders!" The bailiff yelled.

"She is out stealing." Number Nine said trying to be funny. Suddenly, Cathy from Arkansas appeared.

"Your case has been dismissed." The bailiff handed her the pink dismissal letter.

"This is what I went to jail for?" She stated in a questioning tone. Then, Ms. Arkansas left the building. The court appointed counselor circulated the area giving application forms to each individual.

"If you filed an Order of Protection, you need to fill out this form." She said while handing each individual an Order of Protection request. Several Protection Order cases were dismissed. Another lady approached the bailiff.

"What about my Protective Order?" She asked.

"Your Protective Order has been dismissed." The bailiff stated.

"Dismissed?" She said in a baffling tone. "I paid a Process Server. The dude is still out on the streets. I am afraid of him." She said with fear in her eyes. A well-dressed young lady with a head full of weave hanging down to her waist inquired about her Protective Order.

"They haven't said anything to me about my Protective Order," she told her friend.

"Does she need an attorney?" Ms. Weave's friend asked. "I can get her one right now," she said with confidence while slinging her long weave. The Weave Club members devised a plan for securing an attorney. Her friend questioned the bailiff again. "We didn't know that she needed an attorney. She can't represent herself?" She asked.

"Better to have an attorney." The bailiff advised. "Get it Reset." The bailiff informed her about the legal benefits of hiring an attorney. In a flash, a gentleman with a V-shaped toes pointed outward pranced into the Hearing Room. He strutted with swagger in his Steve Harvey style gray suit with the long coat extended to the knees. He wore a stingy-brim black hat with matching black shirt.

"Cat Daddy!" Number Nine yelled aloud while the gentleman strolled into the waiting area.

"That's it, Man! You got good eyes," Cat Daddy said acknowledging the compliment. Cat Daddy promenaded over to his lady friend who sat patiently.

"You gone be alright," he assured her using Ebonics.

"I hope so," she said as Cat Daddy strolled away.

"Take care," Number Nine said as Cat Daddy swiftly left the scene.

"She will be okay," another lady said to Cat Daddy as he left the premises. All of a sudden, Cat Daddy's lady engaged in a verbal altercation with that young lady.

"I'm a grown ass woman, and I don't need anyone to speak for me," she said in a loud harsh tone. Hastily, the Security Guard from Allied Security entered the area.

"Is there a problem?" He asked. No one said a mumbling word.

"Ain't no good luck down here," Cowboy said still complaining. This time he turned his white baseball cap to the right. On the spur of the moment, Cowboy lay down on the bench to take a nap. Attorney Robinson appeared, and he gave Faith instructions.

"If you appear before the judge, request your lawyer and a hearing."

"Okay! Thank you so much for coming. I appreciate you." Faith said scared as hell. On December 16, 2013, Eve talked to the Deputy Sheriff about the Ex-parte Order of Protection.

"I am the victim in a case. I need to talk with the judge. Is approaching the judge's bench allowed?"

"Yes!" The deputy affirmed. "Once all the Protective Orders have been dismissed, you may speak with the judge." Eve entered the courtroom standing on the left while Faith stood on the right. "Mrs. Mimmus, you have a temporary Protective Order against Faith Billingston. Since your temporary Ex-parte Order of Protection was granted, your hearing is scheduled for today."

x

The judge explained. "Do you wish to petition the court for a permanent Ex-parte Protection Order which will be enforced for one year?"

"I don't need an Order of Protection. I will never be able to stop communicating with my daughter for a year. Your Honor, how can I drop the Protective Order?"

"Mrs. Mimmus, I will dismiss the Protective Order. You may continue with a mother and daughter relationship."

"Thank you!" Eve said.

"Momma, I appreciate you." Faith expressed love for her mother. Christmastide loomed during the coldest season of the year. The winter solstice galvanized sentimental family memories. Eve and Faith planned to spend the Christmas holidays together. The day before Christmas Eve united Faith and her mother. Eve gave her daughter a suggestion.

"You need to write a novel about your jail situation." Eve suggested that a story created from their ordeal. Faith experienced the hurdles of life by overcoming adversities which placed stumbling blocks in her path. Her mother knew that one's life is a story, and every antagonist is a character playing a role on the world stage. Hence, Faith painted mental pictures as the chapters of life unfold. As Faith's image reflected in the mirror of life, she gazed into the mirror to undertake a quest to find her inner spirit. While strange consternations ran through her mind, it was peculiar. A quest to find Faith's inner being developed from her genealogy.

"Momma, I'm tired of writing. I want to party, and I want to have plenty of sex like other women. I really haven't had a lot of relationships. My life has been spent teaching and writing novels. My life is an open book." Faith admitted. Eve laughed, and they prearranged the holiday repast by ordering Cajun Dry-Rub wings from Logan's Steakhouse. The manner of preparing food was not a part of their agenda. Eve discussed her immortality.

"I am aging; I had a birthday early in December. I'm blessed to be living at my age. I love you, Faith. I don't want you to be condemned because you went to jail. When I die, don't come to my funeral. People will rake you over blazing flames by finding fault in you. They can be very cruel, and your nemesis will censure you."

"I don't care what people say. I love you, too. You've been a good mother to us. I will sow my respect for you when you die." Faith pledged her commitment to her mother.

"I want you to type a letter to the District Attorney." The following letter was typed:

December 23, 2013

Prosecutor Anita Winbush:

Division 10

Shelby County Government

Memphis, Tennessee

Dear Mrs. Winbush:

I am required to appear in Division 10 on January 9, 2014 for a Domestic Violence Assault case against Mrs. Billingston. I do not wish to prosecute Faith. On December 6, 2013, I appeared in court to express my desire to not prosecute my daughter. At that time, I talked with a court counselor. I am 82 years old. I am not sure that I will live to appear in court. If I die before that date, please honor my request not to prosecute Faith Billingston.

Sincerely,

Mrs. Eve Mimmus

Time set in motion their loving attachment. They reclined in bed hugging each other crying while confessing their love. The family members expressed deep affection by caressing. Eve and Faith decided to seek counseling during their personal crisis. The relationship Counselor advocated asking three questions important to companionships in life. The questions were as follows:

1. Who loves you?
2. Who do you love?
3. Who has your best interest at heart?

The advisor further said.

"You and your mother will have to continue loving each other. Hold steadfast to that love. Your mother is elderly, now. No book has been written about successfully dealing with aging. We learn about aging as we travel through life," the counselor maintained. "When you age some days you wake up, you don't feel well. Other days, you feel just fine." The counselor offered an opinion. The counselor prescribed practical recommendation to resolve the gun issue. The advisor proposed a compromise. He suggested that Faith and her mother give the guns to him for safe keeping. Faith called her Attorney to inform him about the Counselor acting as a mediator.

"Hello Attorney Robinson! My mom and I secured a Counselor." Faith informed her lawyer. "He suggested that we meet in your office to discuss my case. Momma wants to drop the case against me."

"That is nice to get Counseling, but we have to go through the Judicial System to have the felony charges dropped. Your mom has to tell the Prosecutor that she does not wish to pursue the charges herself. That is all she has to say. Faith, you do not have to give up your fire arm to the Counselor or anybody else."

"I will relinquish my weapon to him in order to compromise, but I am a single woman living alone. I will be an easy target for a rapist, a home invader, or murderer." Faith admonished Faith drafted the following compromise, and they signed the document:

I agree to the terms set forth by the Counselor. The Three Step terms were as follows:

1. Guns released to the Counselor at 10:00 A.M. on December 28, 2013.
2. Court Case discussed with the attorney to drop the prosecution.
3. Wills should be made by both parties.

I agree to release my gun to the Counselor in order compromise. However, the resolution to the hand gun issue should have been initiated when Eve Mimmus was asked to relinquish her gun for Faith's safety. The various mood swings from crying, to dying, to disliking, to lying made my living conditions dangerous. My attorney advised me that I am not obligated to give my gun to the Counselor. In good faith, I will release my weapon. Mrs. Eve Mimmus is residing at her residence now. Therefore, my hand gun does not propose a threat to her. Upon consulting with my attorney, the second term should not be initiated. According to Attorney Robinson, the discussion of not prosecuting Faith Billingston should not take place among the four-people listed in the compromise. My attorney stated that this case is in the judicial system. If Eve Mimmus does not wish to prosecute her daughter, she must tell the Prosecutor that desire during the court proceedings on January 27, 2014. I, Faith Billingston, do agree to make a Will. The legal document will show how our worldly goods should be distributed upon our death. Faith called her lover to solicit advice about the documentation of a compromise.

"Hello!" Richie answered.

"Hello, sweetheart! We discussed a compromise during our consultation with the counselor."

"Did you relinquish your weapon?" Richie inquired.

"Yes! I gave my gun to him."

"Did he sign the compromise?" Richie examined.

"Yes! We all signed."

"That's good. How is your writing coming along?" Richie asked.

"I can't concentrate. I am sick of the drama. Shit keeps happening. My life is a fucking open book with one dramatic tale after another."

"I guess all you want is peace," Richie surmised.

"That's all I want, Richie." Faith responded.

"Why not record your thoughts on tape or on the new Voice Recording System?" Richie suggested.

"I've never heard about the Voice Recording System." Faith admitted.

"The Voice Recording System types while you talk. Let's go to Walmart's. I will show you the newest technology." Richie recommended a solution to her writer's block.

"That sounds like a winner. I want to buy a Voice Recording System." The couple visited Walmart's, but the store sold all of their Voice Recording System. Henceforth, Faith continued to utilize her method of writing novels longhand. Writing was therapeutic for her. The literary psychoanalysis method healed Faith's soul. The stream-of-consciousness-novels unlocked the storehouse of memory within Faith's subconscious mind. Writing relieved her mind from the crises and conflicts of life's forces. Life's journey manifested non-fictional events in Faith's existence.

The sum of her experiences unfolded in print. Everybody's story plays on the stage of life. Richie invited Faith to the movie the day after Christmas to see 'Grudge Match'. Upon returning home from the flick, Eve was gone. Faith searched every room calling Eve's name.

"Momma! Momma!" She yelled frantically. "Where in the world is Momma?"

"Where could your mother go at this time of night?" Richie pondered.

"I'll call her house. Maybe, her grandson knows where she disappeared." The phone rang, but they did not answer the landline phone. "I'll call Stan's cell phone." Faith attempted to contact her nephew.

"Richie! He refuses to answer the phone call. I better go over to my mom's house."

"No! Don't go to your mom's house alone. Your legal case is still pending. This seems like a set-up to me. Call the police. Have the police meet you over there." Richie dialed the non-emergency number for the Memphis Police Department.

"Police non-emergency! Officer Blanchard, may I help you?"

"Yes! My friend's mother is missing. She left home, and we don't know her whereabouts. My lady is afraid of approaching her mother because of a pending court case. She needs the police to meet her at the mother's house."

"Sure! An officer will be dispatched to the location. What is the address?"

"The address is 2717 Homer Street. Thank you." Richie said. Two police officers arrived on the scene. Faith was apprehensive about going into the house. The White officer perceived fear in Faith.

"You are really scared of your mother," the man in blue observed.

"Yes! I am afraid of my mom. Her demeanor has changed." Faith insinuated. Stan opened the door before a knock on the door occurred. Eve sat on the couch with a smirk smile on her face.

"I was concerned about your disappearance. I'm glad that you are safe. Y'all take care," Faith said exiting the residence.

"Thank you for coming to help me." Faith said expressing gratitude to the officers.

"You are welcome. Our job is to help citizens in this city," the courteous officer said. The next evening Faith received a call from Eve. Eve left a message on her daughter's Voice Mail Box.

"Faith call me. We need to discuss your case." Faith called her attorney for advice.

"Hello Attorney Robinson! My mother called again. She still wants to discuss the case."

"Faith you shouldn't call her. I'm sure the bond has stipulations about contacting her."

"I want call her back. Attorney Robinson, I need the truth to be exposed. Can I take a Lie Detector Test? I'm not a prevaricator. I want hurt anyone."

"I know you want, Mrs. Billingston. Lie Detector test are not admissible in court. It is best that you stay away from your mother until this case is resolved."

"I'll keep my distance, Attorney Robinson. You are in for the fight of your life with my case. Thank you! Have a good day. Bye!" In a timely fashion, the next Counseling Session leaked valuable information about Eve's gun. The counselor possessed a deep and abiding interest in the circumstances surrounding the gun.

"How did the gun incident start?" The counselor called into question the firearm event.

"I asked momma for her gun, but she refused to give me the weapon. When I got out of jail, I searched in every room for her gun. I couldn't find that gun anywhere." Eve giggled cunningly, and she said.

"I had my gun all the time. I refused to give Faith my gun. My gun was in the Dirty Clothes Hamper. I put my gun under the clothes that needed washing. I hid my gun from my teenage great-grandson. Some boys were bullying him at school. He wanted to defend himself. No one would ever think of looking in the Dirty Clothes Hamper." Everyone laughed.

"Faith, were you distraught about being incarcerated?" The advisor pumped her for an answer.

"No! I wasn't distraught. I gained a spiritual enlightenment in jail. My soul trusted God more while incarcerated." The first day of the calendar year emerged on January 1, 2014. Richie and Faith watched the guitar drop on Beale Street on the television. Since Richie was a profoundly spiritual guy, they prayed. The third day of the New Year generated a train of thoughts in Eve's mind. Eve called her daughter about 10:00 o'clock in the morning.

"How did I get myself in this mess?" Eve requested information about the point in dispute. "I can't wash my clothes. I can't take a bath in this nasty bathtub. Young men are poor housekeepers. Stan doesn't clean up anything. Pray for me," she petitioned Faith. "I feel like I'm getting the Flu."

"I will pray for you momma." Faith promised. "You don't miss a nice home environment until living in a deplorable environment. Our house was never nasty. We kept the house clean. Stan needs to clean-up the house." Faith propounded.

"You are right. I miss having the conveniences in a nice home." Eve mused. She thought meditatively about the life style in the suburbs.

"I miss having you here. I miss being with you so much! Stanley's housekeeping skills are nasty like his mother. Lynn always kept a nasty apartment. He inherited his mother's tendency to keep a nasty house. Nurturing a child through intervention can't overcome nature's hereditary traits." Faith said. On the fourth day of January, Eve called Faith in order to discuss their Wills.

"Faith, have you done your Will? The Counselor suggested that we separate our Wills."

"I need to remove your Nissan from my Will. It is not my place to Will your car to my Executor." Faith reminded Eve.

"I'm not well; I'm sick. I'm just trying to hold on until the 9th of January." Eve said during her dying spell.

"Well! I will accept whatever you decide to put in your Will. Stan already said that he wanted your car when you die." Faith reminded her mother.

"I don't want to hear all that rhetoric." Eve said in a nasty tone. "Bye!"

"I love you," Faith said while hanging up the phone. She realized that her mother didn't want to discuss death. It is cruel for family members to plot the financial benefits for themselves upon the death of a love one. She prayed aloud to her Father. He was the Father who blessed her financially. God was good to Faith. He fought her battle against jealous at work and at church. Through this domestic tragedy, Faith leaned on God. Time crawled at a snail's pace before the court date, but drama proceeded with suspense on a daily basis. Eve telephoned Faith in the morning fussing. Faith refused to explain her point of view with rhetoric. She as not in the mood to argue. He mother left a telephone message on the Voice Mail System. Faith debated whether to return her mom's phone call. She discussed the decision with Richie while cuddling in bed. He had been a trusted friend through the jail ordeal.

"My mom called this morning. She wanted to discuss her Will. She became argumentative. Now, she wants me to call. What should I do? Should I call?"

"Yes! You should call her. Be humble when you talk with her. Don't tell her that I'm over here visiting. She's very possessive of you. She doesn't want you with anybody but herself." Faith dialed her mom's number. Mothers' have an insight into the frailties of men in pursuit of their daughters. Eve wondered if Richie would be good to her daughter.

"Hello momma! I got your message." Faith acknowledged the phone call.

"What did you do today?"

"I went to the grocery store." Faith answered.

"Where is that guy? What is his name?" Eve requested information.

"His name is Richie. I guess he's at home." Faith answered while snuggled next to him.

"Okay!" She said relaxed. Faith hung the phone up, and she made love to Richie. During pillow talk, Richie suggested finding a doctor for her mother. Faith called the Commission on Aging.

"Good morning! This is the Memphis Commission on Aging. Mary speaking!"

"I am having problems with my mother. She shows several different mood swings. She talks bad to me. She dislikes me today, and the next day she loves me. Is this normal?"

"Yes," Mary said. "Don't take it personal."

"I'm glad you explained. Now, I understand that the mood swings are typical for the elderly. She has a great memory, and she is intelligent."

"That is normal." Mary said. "She needs a Geriatric Physician."

"What is a Geriatric Physician?" The type of physician was an important matter of discussion for Faith.

"Geriatric is the branch of medicine that deals with old age. Your mother's insurance company can give you the names of Geriatric Physicians."

"Thanks! I needed this information." Faith called a Geriatric Physician, and she made an appointment for January 15, 2014. On the morning of January 6, 2014, Eve called her daughter at 8:00 A.M.

"Come quick! I need you, now! I'm not feeling well." Eve pleaded.

"I'm on my way. I'll be there as fast as I can." Faith slipped on some clothes, and she rushed to her mom's house. When Faith made her appearance, Eve talked with her concerning Wills.

"I want you to stick with Stanley when I die." Eve stated in a melancholy tone.

"I will, momma. I don't have anything against Stanley. We've had Stan in our family since he was a baby. My problem stems from his family. His mother and sister are against me.

They condemned me all around Orange Mound. I have given them several cars. We provided food, clothes, and shelter for Stanley since birth. His mother never brought him any clothes while he lived with us. She returned our generosity with hatred. Stan accused his Aunt Ida of telling me about the rumors, but she never told me about the gossip. He would be surprised who squealed." Faith escorted her mother to the bedroom to get some clothes for the trip to the hospital.

"Momma, I packed your House Coat and some more items. Where is your money? I gave you $3,700.00 dollars from your bank account. You asked me for your portion of our savings. I know that you paid $500.00 dollars to bail me from jail." Faith asked.

"You are accusing me of stealing her money," Stan's bad conscious blurted defensive remarks. "You ought to be worrying about getting her to the hospital. You are worrying about money whore. I ought to beat your ass!" The big brawny brute attacked Faith in a violent rage. If Stan was concerned about getting Eve to the hospital, he could have driven her to the hospital. He could have called an ambulance service to transport her to the hospital. However, Faith drove from the suburbs of Germantown into Memphis in order to take her mom to the hospital. Faith retaliated back verbally to Stan's threat.

"You better not fuck with me, bitch. Get the fuck out my way. Come on momma! Let's go!"

Eve grabbed $1,900.00 dollars from under her pillow. Se made statement about money.

"I had another stash somewhere." Eve said thinking about her money.

"I'm going to protect you, momma." Stan said.

"Fool! This I my momma. Your momma is the whore's ass you wiggled from at birth. Your momma doesn't know who your daddy is. You are not my brother's son. Your daddy is any trick she fucked down on Mulberry Street." Faith exposed his illegitimate birth.

"He might not be my father. I hate you, whore." He said. "Bitch, you ain't nothing but a whore."

"Your momma is the whore, punk! Your momma fucked every trick on the Track when she prostituted on Mulberry. You are a trick baby. In fact, your momma had six illegitimate children. She ain't never been married. Go protect your real grandmother. Your grandmother is a low-class café. She is a stone alcoholic."

"Whore!" He yelled. "I ain't never liked you." Stan admitted his disdain for Faith.

"I'm a good whore." Faith bragged about her skills. "I ain't a poor whore. Move Punk!"

"Stan! You are wrong for calling Faith a whore. She was married. She has dated men. In each relationship, she dated the guy for years. You've never seen a lot of different men visiting her."

Eve chastised Stan in Faith's defense. Faith took her mother to the Emergency Room. They assigned Eve to the Observation Room for 48 hours. They checked Eve from head to toe. Dr. Owens diagnosed her heart rate, blood pressure, and they gave her an EKG. Faith noticed a question mark on the machine. She went to the nurse's station.

"What does the question mark mean?" She asked the nurse.

"The question mark is not a danger sign. Your mom's heart rate has slowed down to 58, but that is normal. We read the patient not the machine. When you sleep, your heart rate slows down because of inactivity. If you have any questions, feel free to ask me." The nurse said. After 48 hours of observation, Eve as released from the hospital. On January 9, 2014, Faith located Attorney Robinson near Division 10.

"Is that your mother in the wheelchair?" Attorney Robinson asked.

"Yes! She is my mother." Faith informed him about her maternal relationship.

"You ought to be ashamed of yourself assaulting that sweet little old lady. I am disappointed in you. How could you mistreat your mother? This is disgusting." The attorney scorned Faith's actions.

"Whose side are you representing? You are supposed to be my lawyer. If you don't want to represent me, I can hire another lawyer." Faith warned. She selected this attorney based on his Law Firm's slogan about helping good people in a bad situation. Faith was a good person in a bad situation.

"I will represent you, Faith. I am your lawyer. I have taken your case, and I am going to work with you to the end of your case." Attorney Robinson assured Faith of his legal duties. "I'm going to the Investigation Room to check on your case. I will return shortly," the attorney said. Eve and Faith marked time talking until the lawyer returned.

"Come here!" Eve beckoned Faith to lean over close to her. "You are living your book," she whispered. "You are playing a role. The incident with Stan is a role in your book. Everything happens for a reason." Eve justified the events logically. Momentarily, Attorney Robinson returned.

"I got some good news, and I got some bad news." Faith's eyes bucked in shock. "The good news is you can go home, now. You are a nice lady, Faith. You really don't belong down here. Look around you. You don't look like these criminals waiting on their court cases. Now, the bad news is that they have to investigate your gun. The state has a Gun Down Program, and all weapons are checked. Guns are checked in order to reveal if the weapon has been used in the commission of a crime. A grant pays funds for the Gun Down Program. Memphis Gun Down tracks violence, and a report is given to the mayor every three months. The program has reduced youth gun violence. Youth violence has dropped tremendously." Attorney Robinson ascertained.

"Your court case is postponed until January 27, 2014. Try to enjoy your day." On the spur of the moment, Eve suggested taking a joyride through Orange Mound.

I want to see my family home. Drive through the Mound." Nostalgia overwhelmed Eve with a longing to return to former happy circumstances. Driving down Clover Street, they saw an unusual situation in a Black neighborhood. Two White men stood in a neighbor's yard chatting.

"Did you see those White folks standing in Mrs. Atkin's yard?" Faith asked.

"Drive around the corner. I don't believe some White folks are living in Orange Mound." Faith drove around the corner turning left on Neil Street driving back to Clover Street.

"I'm going to ask them why they are in Orange Mound." Pulling in front of Mrs. Atkin's house, Faith greeted the young men. "Hi! I'm Faith. I grew-up here. I lived at 775 Clover." Faith said while pointing at the house. "My mother and I were surprised to see some White folks in a Black neighborhood."

"I'm Justin, and I bought this house." He informed Faith.

"Why did you select Orange Mound as a place of residence? This is a historically Black neighborhood."

"I'm Doctor Justin Pearson. This is Doctor Delaware Davis. We work at the Community Health Care Clinic. We wanted to live in the community with our patients attending the Health Care Clinic."

"I'm Delaware, and I live across the Street." He said while pointing toward Eve's childhood home.

"My grandfather built the house you're living in now."

"Would you like to see your family home?" Delaware offered a tour of the house that Big Daddy built.

"Yes! We haven't been inside of our house since Momma sold the house to Mrs. Henderson." Touring Eve's family home, she reminisced about childhood memories.

Chapter 7.

THE DAY OF ATONEMENT

The Day of Atonement arrived on January 27, 2014. The reparation for Faith's wrongdoing allowed reconciliation between mother and daughter. The court case provided a means for making amends for a wrongdoing inflicted on Eve. Faith and Eve met a God-sent couple in the parking lot. Betty and Charles were Angels. Charles volunteered to push Eve's wheelchair into the Criminal Justice Center while Betty directed them into the Handicap entrance. As they walked toward the Criminal Justice Center, Betty made the following statement:

"I helped my mother in a wheelchair until she passed."

"I'm trying to learn how to deal with the elderly, but I'm not doing a good job."

"You'll learn," Betty said encouraging Faith. Once inside of the Judicial System, Faith moved to the elevator. However, she didn't know how to descend down to the Second floor. A gentleman from Support Services recognized her confusion.

"Where are you going, ma'am?"

"We are appearing in Division 10." Faith answered.

"Follow me!" The Support Service employee took them through a private door.

"This is the Judge's elevator, but I'm going to let you go to court on their elevator."

"I thank God for you. God is really working today." Eve said gratefully.

"He always works for us," the service man said.

"I'm glad that he put you in our path today." Faith praised. Division 10 heard Domestic Violence cases. Several people gathered waiting for court to open at 9:00 A.M. on January 27, 2014. Faith sat next to a couple distraught about the predicament their daughter found herself with the Criminal Justice Center.

"I believe our daughter accidently backed into his car, the father said justifying his daughter's vehicular crash. "She had to be high when she hit his car." "She should take the case straight to the Grand Jury. Her case should fare better with twelve people. One of those jurors would understand her plight, and it would be thrown out of court. Our children like messing around with low life people. When you dance around the crab barrel, a crab will pull you into the barrel." The mother expressed her thoughts.

The period of time before Division 10 allowed friends to congregate.

"Hey man! I hate to stare, but didn't we play basketball together."

"Yeah man! I played for Woodhaven."

"I played with that team, too. I thought that your face looked familiar. They are making plenty of money down here. Fines, court cost, and lawyer fees are making big bucks for the Criminal Justice Center."

"They've been wearing me out. I spent $4,000.00 dollars on court fees. My wife lied on me."

"Check this out! They take the woman's word," his friend said. "The Domestic Violence case is worse than a dope charge."

"You ought to be able to talk stuff out with your spouse when you've been together that many years." As they continued sitting in the lobby, Faith saw a white-haired, blue eyed, well-dressed attorney with a beige suit, a pair of tan Ostrich Skin Cowboy boots walking with his client. Eavesdropping on their conversation, Faith heard an unknown slang terminology.

"I'm a Hook. He's a GD." The client used an unknown slang terminology that the attorney didn't understand.

What's a Hook?" The Attorney asked.

"It's a gang member. I'm a Vice Lord. I let him know that I was a Vice Lord." The client bragged.

"Mr. Simmons, I believe that she is going to try to poison the judge against you." The lawyer surmised.

"She's involved with all of those gang members." He said as they walked down the hall. In reality, the Willie Lynch Method is still dividing Black men today. The Willie Lynch method describes using one Black man against another Black man. African-Americans are killing Blacks in the name of gang rivalry. Gang members lynch people of their own race using 380 Automatics., 9 Millimeters, and Uzi's to strangle the life from a brother. The Vice Lords verses the Gangster Disciples shows a new form of Lynching in the 21st century. The Ku Klux Klan's noose faces retirement now. Black men are killing each other using red and blue bandanas as a noose. In the 21st century, African-Americans lynch fellow Blacks at a greater magnitude than the Ku Klux Klan. In the interim before court convened, the lady who distributes brochures on a daily basis turned the corner near Eve. She always displayed a friendly disposition.

"God told me to tell you that you want have to come back down here anymore. Let God handle this situation for you." She advised. Suddenly, she looked at Faith, and she said.

"You have a Happy New Year, ma'am."

"You too," Faith said. Division 10 opened, and the people entered the courtroom.

The sheriff directed the people into the courtroom. He informed everyone about the seating arrangements.

"If you have a lawyer, you must sit on the right side of the court room. If you do not have a lawyer, you must sit on the left side of the court room." The people without a lawyer signed a list to be assigned a Public Defender. "Turn your cell phone off completely. Do not put your cell phone on vibrate." The bailiff requested. "You will be charged $100.00 dollars if your phone goes off."

"Is the bailiff for real?" Eve asked Faith in surprise. "Is my phone going to ring?" Eve questioned.

"Let me turn your phone off." Faith offered to turn her mother's phone off completely. During the interval, a young lady entered. The bailiff asked.

"Do you have a subpoena, ma'am?"

"Yes," she replied.

"Stand outside." The bailiff stated. "You can't come into the courtroom now." The bailiff busily directed people into the proper criminal channels.

"You got a case," he asked a young lady walking briskly through the door.

"My case has been dismissed," she said proudly.

"Go down to LL 81. You have to pay court cost," the bailiff said. "When you go to LL 81, get a piece of paper, and bring it back to him," Officer Patterson said pointing to a gentleman. "If you don't, it will stay on your record. Make sure it doesn't happen no more." The sheriff said.

"All rise!" Sheriff Patterson said. "Honorable Judge Henry Thompson is presiding." The judge occupied his seat in front of a gold circular plaque with the Roman Numeral XVI ascribed across the top. Under the Roman Numerals, the words Agriculture and Commerce were printed in capital letters with the year 1796 imprinted on the state's medallion. The Great Seal of The State of Tennessee was inscribed around the plaque in bold capital letters.

"You are here for the state of Tennessee. When you come forth, your case will be heard," the judge informed the people. The court of Domestic Relations revealed patriotism to one's state and country by displaying an American flag with stars and strips along with the State of Tennessee's red flag with a navy-blue circle adorned with three white stars. During the span of time, a Public Defender called the two people in need of a lawyer. Occurring at the right time, the inmates from Jail East entered the courtroom. They were seated next to the judge's bench. The bailiff called the first inmate.

"Number 40! Johnny Wallace step forward." The bailiff commanded him to appear. The male inmates wore dark navy-blue jail attire.

"You are charged with Domestic Violence assault with bodily harm. You assaulted Angela Gardner. Stay away from her home. No contact!" The judge said forcefully. "If you violate your bail condition, your bond will be increased. You must not harass, annoy, contact or otherwise communicate with her. You cannot contact her directly or indirectly. You must stay away from any location where she might be found. You are prohibited from carrying a gun. You must reframe from using drugs or consuming alcohol. These are provisions of your bond." The judge warned the criminal.

"Number 23!" The bailiff called. The convict stood before the judge.

"You are charged with aggravated assault. You are facing 3 to 15 years if convicted. You have the right to a Preliminary hearing. You are prohibited from carrying a gun.

You must reframe from using drugs or consuming alcohol. Stay away from the victim," the judge demanded." These are the provisions of your bond." The judge stated.

"Number 38! Brenda Lawson step forward." The bailiff ordered. Brenda stood before the judge dressed in bright orange jail attire.

"You are charged with aggravated assault and vandalism. You are facing 11 months and 29 days in jail. Do you have a Tennessee Handgun Permit?"

"No sir!" The inmate answered.

"You are not permitted to have a firearm. Drugs and alcohol are forbidden. You must not violate your bond. Your bond is set at sixty thousand dollars. Can you make bond?" The judge questioned.

"Yes sir!" She answered.

"Stay away from him." The distinguish judge ordered.

"Number 45! Grace," the bailiff said.

"You are charged with Domestic Assault and drug possession." The judge presented the allegations against the inmate. "You're facing 11 months and 29 days for drugs.

Your bond is set at four thousand dollars. You have a fifty-dollar Administration fee." The judge stated.

"Number 12! Gregory Wilson." The bailiff summoned.

"Have you got a bond, yet?" The dignified white-haired judge asked.

"Not that I know off." Answered the inmate. "I may bond out Monday." He said hoping inwardly for bond money.

"Number 54!" The bailiff called Benjamin Bolden.

"Is anyone going to bond you out soon?" The judge asked.

"No!"

"You need to pay fifty dollars Administration Fee." The judge set a dollar amount for using public services.

"Number 101!" The bailiff summoned that inmate's number to the judge's bench.

"You are charged with violation of Probation. You could serve 11 months and 29 days in jail. Your bond is set at $15,000.00 dollars. Are you going to bond out?" The judge inquired.

"Yes!" The inmate answered affirmatively.

"You must appear in court on February 8, 2014. Bring your lawyer with you." The judge advised. In mare Number 100 was called to approach the bench.

"Nicholas Davis, you are charged with Domestic Assault with bodily harm. You are facing 11 months and 29 days in jail. Mr. Davis, you have appeared before this court seven times in the last year. You must not harass, annoy, contact or communicate with her. You cannot contact her directly or indirectly. You must not appear in any location where she might be visiting. No contact!" The judge ordered.

"Stay away from her home! Your bail conditions forbid you from having a firearm or using drugs or alcohol. Will you be able to arraign out of jail?"

"No sir!" the convict answered.

"I will appoint a Public Defender to handle your case. You must pay a fifty-dollar Administration Fee." A young man about 25 years old sat next to Faith. He sparked up a conversation.

"Where do I know you from? Do you know my mom? Her name is Mrs. Sanders."

"No," Faith answered. "I don't know Mrs. Sanders." All of a sudden, he pulled his cell phone out of his pocket. He began to move his fingers across the screen on the phone.

"You better put your phone away," Faith warned. The bailiff walked over to the young man, and he said.

"Stop playing with your phone!" The bailiff demanded. He gave the bailiff a thumb's up, and he placed the phone in his pocket. Suddenly, the young man's lawyer called him outside the court room. When he returned, Faith asked him a question.

"What school did you attend?"

"I attended Castle High," he answered proudly.

"I know you from Castle High School. I was your teacher." Faith said.

"I remember your face." He confessed. A slim, dark-skinned young lady with a long Remy weave and eight-inch heels with gold nail heads on the heel approached the judge's bench.

"You are charged with a Violation of a Protection Order. You have the right to a jury trial. Do you wave your right?

"I plead guilty," she answered.

"Are you voluntarily pleading guilty?"

"Yes," she assured the judge.

"You've got to spend on day in jail, but you've already spent one day in jail. Time served," the judge said. Instantaneously, Faith's student said.

"Let me out! That's my lady." He quickly exited the court room fast tracking behind her. Without a warning, Faith's lawyer approached her.

"Sit tight!" Attorney Robinson instructed. "It took forever to talk to an investigator. Now, I'm going to talk with the Prosecutor."

"Okay!" Faith answered. "Keep me posted on my case," she said. Attorney Robinson returned, and he said.

"The Prosecutor will talk with your mother." An elderly lady from the District Attorney's office pushed Eve's wheelchair into a private room adjacent to the court room. The Prosecuting Attorney with long white hair, wire-rimmed glasses, and a blue pants suit job entailed bringing crooks to justice. The DA was determined to render a judgment.

"Hello, Mrs. Eve Mimmus. I'm Diane Carter. As the Prosecuting Attorney, I bring to trial Domestic Violence assault cases. I'm calling into question the gun incident with your daughter. Did Faith point the gun at you on the day in question?" The prosecutor attempted to pump answers from Eve.

"No! Faith laid her gun on the bed. Then, she asked me for my gun. I didn't understand why she wanted my gun. I've had my gun for 10 years. I refused to give her my weapon."

"Let me call into question the police report." The Prosecutor pursued answers. "You stated that Faith pulled the gun on you several times." The counsellor at law grilled Eve extensively.

"I lied!" Eve confessed to prevaricating about facing the barrel of a gun. "Her actions discombobulated me. My nerves were flustered, and I was scared." The Prosecutor's quest for interlocking statements failed.

"Why did your daughter want your gun?" The legal practitioner quizzed.

"According to Faith, she wanted to put the gun in a Lock Box. I'm from the old school. Faith should have explained her motives to me. We discussed our legal ordeal, and we could have solved this issue in a better way. I love my daughter, and she loves me." Meanwhile, a group of ladies babbled continuously in the back of the court room. They chattered non-stop. Finally, the bailiff walked to the area of the chit chat.

"No talking! Don't talk too much in court. Y'all are talking too much in court." The sheriff scolded the loquacious jokers about disrupting court procedures. During the interval, Faith sat anxiously wondering about the discussion between the Prosecutor and Eve. At that moment, the Prosecutor confronted Faith.

"You can get your mom," she said in an amicable tone.

"Thank you!" Faith said pleasantly. At that moment, she entered the conference room, and she rolled Eve's wheelchair into Division 10 for arraignment.

"Where did that woman go, girl?" Eve asked speaking in reference to the Prosecutor. "She is tough!"

"She is up front at the Judge's bench." Faith answered.

In the meantime, a Public Defender called his client to approach the bench.

"Where is your witness?"

"All three of y'all are witnesses?" The Public Defende asked surprised.

"Raise your hand. Do you swear and affirm to tell the truth?" Each witness stated in unison.

"I do!"

"Who are you going to question first." The Judge asked.

"I'll begin with this witness first." He turned toward the other witnesses, and he said.

"Stand outside the courtroom. We will call for you later." The lawyer retrieved information from the first witness.

"State your name."

"Sharon Barnes.!"

"How long have you known the defendant?"

"I've known her three years."

"Where were you last weekend?" The lawyer interrogated the witness.

"I was at 2230 Austin."

"Do you live in that location?"

"Yes!"

"How long have you lived at that residence?"

"I've been living there about three months." The witness answered.

"Who all was in the house the night of the incident?"

"Me, Candice, Brenda, Erica and the children were in the house." The witness gave an account of everybody present that night.

"What did Candice say to her children?"

"She told the children to stop running around the house before get hurt."

"Where was everybody else?"

"They were in the Living Room talking."

"How long did everybody stay up talking?"

"They were still talking around four o'clock."

"Did you witness any violent action in the house?"

"I heard a scream."

"What did you after a scream?"

"After hearing the scream, I went to the back of the house. I heard Tiffany ask her momma to stop hitting her."

"What happened then?"

"After a while, she stopped. I didn't hear anything else.

"Where were the other children?

"The kids were in the Living Room."

"Did Tiffany come out of the room after two o'clock in the morning?"

"No sir!"

"Did Candice explain where Tiffany was at the time?"

"No sir! She was in the room by herself. Candice said that's my child; I can let her sleep."

"Did you see any injuries? Were bruises the extent of her injuries?"

"She didn't have any bruises." The witness said.

"You don't know what you heard. How can you say that she wasn't injured? You didn't witness anything." The lawyer cast doubt on the witness statement.

"I heard some slapping."

"This is Probable Cause!" The lawyer stated adamantly. "Your case is dismissed for Non-Probable Cause. You are free to go." The young lady accused of child abuse quickly left the courtroom. In the nick of time, Faith's lawyer beckoned her outside the courtroom.

"Your case has been dismissed. You are free to go, but you have to pay court cost. Go to LL81."

"

"Will they take a check?"

"They don't take checks; they take cash or credit cards."

"How much is court cost?"

"Since you spent a couple of nights in jail, you will pay about $200.00 dollars."

"Wow! A room at the Peabody would cost about $100.00 dollars a night." Her lawyer laughed, and he said.

"They are in the middle of a trial. Go to LL 81, and they will give you a payment schedule. You are a nice lady Mrs. Billingston."

"Thank you, Attorney Robinson." When Faith returned to the courtroom, the Judge summoned her to approach the bench.

"In the interest of justice, your case has been dismissed. You must pay your fine. If you don't pay Court Cost the State of Tennessee will take your Driver's License." Faith's slate was officially clean. She didn't have a criminal record.

"I'll pay the Court Cost." Faith assured the Judge. Then, she turned to her lawyer and said.

"You are a good lawyer. Thank you." Eve and Faith left the Criminal Justice Center in order to live life lovingly and peacefully. As they exited the building, they overheard a conversation among a young man and two young ladies.

"A close mouth doesn't get fed." He stated to the girls.

"I cam down here to get you. Where is my gas money?" The lady driver asked.

"What gas money?" She asked in a questioning statement. "I told you that I didn't have any money."

"No money! You are a weak bitch. You are a poor ass bitch, and I ain't riding no bitch free. You were out there last night prostituting. You should've gotten some money. I'm gone!" She left her friend standing outside the Criminal Justice Center., and she split the scene. Eve and Faith decided to dine at Longhorn Steak House. The hostess escorted them to a booth.

"I'm glad that you are out of jail. I didn't want to see you suffer in a jail cell for years, but you needed time-out. I can't spank you because you're grown. You are still my child, and I needed to discipline you. I love you, and I always will." Eve explained.

"I love you too, Momma! I understand. I'm happy that my case was dismissed, and I don't have a criminal record. Incarceration feels like slavery. The Deputy Sheriff Overseer tells you when to eat, when to sleep, when to shower, and when to socialize with other inmates." Faith described the living conditions in the penal system.

"I objected to your relationship with Richie for your benefit. He is a widower, and he has been involved with several women since the death of his wife. I don't want you to waste your time in a relationship without a commitment. You are not getting any younger. Men like Rich live by a certain philosophy." Eve said.

"What philosophy is that, Momma?" Faith questioned.

"One life: one wife is some widowers' philosophy about marriage. You deserve better. You must be strong, Faith. We have a strong family genealogy originating from Ethiopia." Eve revealed their family's heritage.

"Did Mammy's parent come from Ethiopia?" Faith inquired.

"Yes! My cousin, Ontibile, discussed our family's history in depth with Mammy. In fact, Mammy gave Ontibile her African name. Ontibile means 'God is watching over me'. We praise God for watching over our family's safe journey across the virtual waterway of the Red Sea to America." Eve revealed the etymology of her cousin's name.

"How long did the voyage take for our ancestors to reach America?"

"The voyage took six to eight weeks, but inclement weather made the journey longer." Eve recounted the time element for the slaves' trip to the New World. Continuing, she says. "Slave trading was a lucrative business in Ethiopia during the 18th century." Eve disclosed.

"How is our family's bloodline linked to Ethiopia?"

"Ontibile is our family's historian. She listened to Mammy's narration of past events. Our great-grandfather lived in Oroma. Our family tree is connected to royalty. Emperor Menelik II's mother was born in Oroma before becoming a Court servant in the Solomon Dynasty. Menelik II's birth into the highest social stratification of Ethiopian royalty linked his heritage to the Queen of Sheba." Eve said tracing the family's lineage.

"How did the patriarch of our family become a slave?" Faith asked.

"According to Ontibile, the leadership role changed every 8 years in Oroma. The Borara nobles from the highest strata raided the Oroma neighborhood for slaves. In the Horn of Africa, slavery was legal in Ethiopia. When the new leader took office, he selected several Red skin Oroma youth for slavery. Red Oroma slaves with a lighter pigment had a higher value than Black Oroma slaves. The difference in value of slaves based on skin color existed in Africa long before the Willie Lynch method in America. Africans used the differences in hereditary characteristics of Negros based on color, mentality, social status, and age to classify people. Racism in Ethiopia discriminated against the barya subculture of ethnic minorities. Ten to 16-year-old boys were worth more to the slave trade. Grandpa Berihum and Grandma Aamina connected on Ma Stick's plantation. The Oromaic language united our great-great grandparents. They were not obboleessa and obboleetti which means brother and sister in our Ethiopian language. Mammy was conceived from this union. Berihum, meaning 'let him guide us' in Ethiopia, revealed our grandparents' mission for the family's freedom." Eve documented the family's history.

"I'm glad to be free from the Bluff City Criminal Justice Center," Faith said.

"You were born into a family of intelligent Ethiopians. I flashed back to the past to guide you to a successful future. I'm going to slip away from you, God has called my soul

Home. I'm leaving you because I'm going to die soon."

"Don't leave me, Momma! Don't leave me here with these cruel, jealous people. I will be all alone." Faith said crying.

"You want be alone. You've got God. I want you to love everybody." Eve gave Faith instructions on living life successfully.

"Loving people who've mistreated you is a difficult task."

"Faith! You must forgive them, and you must love them anyway. How can you show love to everybody?" Eve asked.

"I can devise a plan to save lives." Faith plotted a scheme to show love.

"When you save a person's life, you give the ultimate form of love. How do you plan to save people's lives?"

"I have a proposal to submit to the Bluff City Council. I found a Preparedness Grant for the renovation of old Wildcat's Den High School. The Intergovernmental Affairs Specialist e-mailed me the notice of funding information. Bryan Simpson is aware of my interest in the Homeland Security Grant Program. I'll present the proposal at the next Bluff City Council meeting.

"Wildcat's Den High School's legacy dates back to 1940's. My sister, Lily, marched in the first graduating class from Wildcat's Den in 1946." Eve continued documenting the history of the school. "All of your family members graduated from the Den: your dad, his sisters, his brother, and his friends. Wildcat's Den is a family tradition for all to the residents of Orange Mound. We are proud to have that old building placed on the National Register of Historic places. Your proposal will be the greatest gift of love to the Orange Mound Community. When is the next Bluff City Council meeting?" Eve asked inspiring Faith to speak before the council.

"The next meeting is September, 2015," Faith gave the date.

"You need to present your idea at that meeting." Faith prepared to present her proposal to the Council on September,2015. Faith entered the Federal Building placing her purse on the table to be inspected by the Police Officer. The speaker walked through the whole-body imaging device used for detecting objects concealed underneath a person's clothing.

The Millimeter Wave Scanner cleared her o proceed into the Council Chamber. Prayer was the starting point for the Bluff City Council meeting. The council members communed with God while a female preacher delivered a prayer.

"Madam Controller, please call the roll," the Chairman requested. In a logical sequence after the prayer, a list of council members' names was called to check attendance.

"Mr. Chairman, you have a quorum," the Controller stated.

"Great! We have a quorum," the Chairman revealed with pleasure. "We have the number of members required to transact the business of the city." Continuing, he asked. "Can someone read the minutes from our last meeting?" Councilwoman Jordan read the minutes

"Mr. Chairman! I read the minutes, and I approve." The Councilwoman accepted the minutes.

"I second the approval of the minutes," Councilman Wallace endorsed the minutes.

"The minutes have been moved and properly second by Mr. Wallace." Chairman Boykins uttered. The council commenced with item on the agenda. Councilwoman Pauline Jordan presented items on the agenda concerning a grant for Bluff City Energy. As an employee of Bluff City Energy, Councilwoman Jordan worked diligently to approve all proposals for the electricity dispensed to the citizens of the

Bluff City. Bluff City Energy received millions of dollars in grant funds to help poor citizens. However, the Bluff City Council members approved adding one dollar to all customers' bills to help the less fortunate. Since grant money was awarded to help citizens pay their electricity bill, where would the customer one dollar be spent each month? The Controller called for the second item on the agenda. The world renown Beale Street required approval for regulations to protect tourist and citizens of the Bluff City. The Council Chairman's entrepreneurship in Real Estate investments gave him a vested interest in Beale Street. However, his real estate dealings did not propose a conflict of interest. The Beale Street ordinance passed unanimously. Chairman Boykin opened the meeting to citizens with presentations to Bluff City Council.

"If you guys care to speak on any item, please come up and grab a comment card from our Sergeant-at-arms," Chairman Boykins said. Continuing with the instructions, the councilman elaborated. "Write your name and address for the record. We will call you up when the item appears on the agenda." Faith approached the Sergeant-at-arms to secure a comment card.

"May I have a card, please?"

"You've got something to tell them. I know you have an Issue to present to the council," the police officer functioning as the Sergeant-at-arms.

"Lawrence Dickins, 1219 Mason Street." The ivory skin tone orator with a white beard greeted the council members. "I'm here to speak about the Confederate statue. The Confederate statues in the Bluff City were erected as a symbol of White supremacy over Black people. These statues honor men who fought to keep Black people in slavery. As long as these Confederate statues remain, the concept of racial bigotry will remain in the minds of Americans. Today, many White people march with Black protestors because of a guilt complex from the sins of our forefathers during slavery."

"Thank you, sir." Chairman Boykins said. The chairman called the second speaker.

"Johnathon Sampson approach the podium."

"My name is Johnathon Sampson. I live at 4957 Burnett Drive in Millington, Tennessee. I'm her to speak about the monuments. The Nathan Bedford Forrest, Jefferson Davis, Abraham Lincoln, WC Handy, Thomas Jefferson, and Martin Luther King statues were erected to document historical people in our nation. Some of these statuesque images have been targets of attack. The city has more important issues to attack rather than the removal of Confederate Monuments. While you spend valuable taxpayer's money talking about the removal of Nathan Bedford Forrest and Jefferson Davis statues, people in this city are dying daily. The murder rate is at an all time high. The new media reports crime, poverty, rape, corruption and murder every day. These are the issues facing the citizens in this city. Yet, the police and firemen are understaffed. A vast majority of police officers left the Bluff City for better paying police jobs elsewhere. Instead of solving the issues in the Bluff City, you've wasted millions of taxpayers' money on legal fees to remove the Confederate statues. The money spent on Nathan and Jefferson could have been paid for salaries to the police officers and firemen."

The Council Chairman refused to give a receptive sign for the ideas presented about the Confederate monuments. The speaker discourse about the importance of historical monuments upset the African-American chairman Council Chairman Boykins smiled with a smirk while making a sarcastic remark.

"Thank you, sir! Your two minutes have ended."

Looking serious now with a stern look, Chairman Boykins said. "You can take the Nathan Bedford Forrest and Jefferson Davis statues back to Millington where you live." The Caucasian speaker exited the Council Chamber. At that point, Dr. Franklin Edwards leaned toward the chairman whispering in his ear while the microphone echoed his statement.

"Billingston is here." Dr. Edwards respectfully made Faith's presence known. Faith worked with Dr. Edwards at Centerville High School for years. She admired his level five score on the states standardize test, and she aspired to move from her level four statue to the highest level of the state's test. City Councilman, Dr. Franklin Edward, was a member of the most powerful Black political professionals in the Bluff City.

"Faith Billingston, 7707 Randle Lane, Memphis, Tennessee." She followed the protocol of revealing one's place of residence. "I am presenting a proposal from LIFT which is an acronym for Learning Involves Further Training. LIFT request permission to receive Preparedness Grant for the Orange Mound Community. The Preparedness Grant provides funding to improve America's readiness in protecting our communities against attacks like North Korea. The grant enables communities to develop a readiness plan to protect citizens against terrorists' attacks. The grant reflects the governments focus on funding for program that ensure public safety. The FEMA grant program helps address evolving nuclear threats by providing the whole Orange Mound

Community with maximized preparedness by renovating Wildcat's Den High School located on Dallas Avenue. Wildcat's Den was built in 1914. The urban area of Orange Mound faces the most significant threat from an Intercontinental Ballistic missile released towards the United States Mainland. With Homeland Security Funding, a large Bomb Shelter would be constructed in the Wildcat's Den building to offer protection for members of the Orange Mound community when a nuclear threat arises. The FEMA Preparedness Grant allows $1,000,000 million dollars for project construction. Recipients using funds for construction projects must comply with the Davis-Bacon Act. The statues of John George Deaderick and Izey Eugene Meacham will be placed on the Wildcat's Den High School's campus to give honor to White men responsible for African-American families home ownership. Members of the Black Lives Matter movement will probably object to the statue of White men being erected in a predominantly Black neighborhood. However, Orange Mound would cease to exist without the Real Estate deals between John Deaderick and Izey Meachum. The Bluff City Administration maintained that the city no longer owned Wildcat's Den High School. Faith, then, presented the proposal to Bluff City School District's Department of Grants.

Yes! Racism exists. The mayor of the Bluff City presented a waiver to the Historical Commission of Tennessee to remove the Confederate statues in an attempt to eliminate civil unrest in the city. We must use the past as a guide to the future. History not revealed kills the intellectual life of past events which paves a path to present events leading to the future success of a nation. The Civil War of 2017 seeks to remove the symbols of bigotry and racism. After the historical Confederate statues are removed from the South, Black Lives Matter should embark upon a mission to remove the hatred indoctrinated in the mind-set of African-Americans by the Willie Lynch method. Black people are killing other African-Americans in neighborhoods across the United State. Every week Blacks lynch other Negros with 9-millimeter metal nooses. Our next movement as African-Americans is to stop the Black on Black crime sweeping through our country. America's battle is not Black people against White people. Our battle is against North Korea. In the eyes of Kim Jong Un, we are all Yankees in American. To Kim Jong Un, it does not matter if our forefathers fought for the Union Army or Confederate Army aYankee bastards. He vowed to send the Yankee bastards a gift delivering a hail of fire to America. American's should focus on preparing the citizens for a Nuclear Bomb attack by revealing the location of Bomb Shelters in each city or build Safe Room Bomb Shelters in the United States.

About The Authors

The authors created a fictionalized character in The Strain of Shackles in honor of their families real Slave Master. Master Richard Dick Jones was born to Fanning Jones and Polina Jones in 1845. Master Richard Dick Jones from Panola County, Mississippi owned the authors' great-great Grandparents as slaves. Faith's lineage stems from Sally Jones. Sally Jones was born in 1877 to Mammy. Richard Dick Jones bloodline ran through the DNA of Sally Jones Bobo. She exemplified the strength and determination to succeed. Grandma Sally Jones' intellectual strength educated her four daughters with a college degree from Mississippi Industrial College. Her daughter Lois taught school. Lois Greenwood was employed as a teacher in the Mt. Olive Public School System in Tunica, Mississippi. Her salary was fixed at $17.50 per month. Teachers' Licenses were issued only after passing a test. In 1934, Madea was issued a License to teach the First Grade. Madea gained a Teachers' Licence in 1935 to teach the Third Grade. Superintendent West issued Lois Greenwood another Teachers' License in 1936. Madea's salary increased to $30.00 dollars per month before moving to Memphis, Tennessee. Madea was proud of her sister Selma Bennett's position as the principal of Dundee Elementary School.Grandma Sally Jones Bobo's sister Aunt Lou Jones gave birth to a musically talented son. Compton Jones' musical talent used an African Ancestry instrument to make music. The Diddley Bow was made out of wire allowing the struck of the of the musicians finger to play sounds by sliding a bottleneck up and down the wire. The Jones' musical clan consisted of Virgie Jones, Annie Jones and Melvin Jones. Compton Jones published a song in special recognition to Master Richard Dick Jones. "Old Dick Jones Is Dead and Gone" is sold on Amazon.com. today. Our family is grateful to David Evans for the Copyright of Afro-American Music in the Library of Archive of Folk Culture. Compton Jones' musical talent will forever be remembered on the Library of Archive of Folk Culture.